Shadow Dancing

OTHER BOOKS BY THIS AUTHOR

Zimbabwe Spin: Politics and Poetics. Ka`a`awa, HI: Pacific Raven Press, 2015.

Love's Seasons: Generations Genetics Myths. Ka`a`awa, HI: Pacific Raven Press, 2014.

Timmy Turtle Teaches. Children's book. Ka`a`awa, HI: Pacific Raven Press, 2012.

Frank Marshall Davis: The Fire and the Phoenix (A Critical Biography). Ka`a`awa, HI: Pacific Raven Press, 2012.

Tourmalines: Beyond the Ebony Portal. Ka`a`awa, HI: Pacific Raven Press, 2010.

*Pacific Raven: Hawai`i Poems.* Ka`a`awa, HI: Pacific Raven Press, 2009. (Winner of 2010 American Book Award from the Before Columbus Foundation.)

New and Collected Poems. Berkeley, CA: Ishmael Reed Publishing, 2003.

Oral Histories of African Americans. Interviews by Kathryn Waddell Takara. Center for Oral History. Social Science Research Institute. Honolulu, HI: University of Hawai`i at Mānoa, 1990.

CREDITS

"The Advancing Day Reveals." ["Under Beijing Skies"]. *The Bamboo Muse: Art, Prose, Poetry,* edited by Alonzo Davis. Amherst, VA: Virginia Center for the Creative Arts, 2010.

"China Stones." ["Imperial Steps and Stones"]. *Chaminade Literary Review* (Spring 1998).

"Fragrance in Moonlight." *Qingdao Daily* (July 2011).

"Qingdao." ["Blossoming Beauty"]. *Qingdao Literature* (1997).

"The Public PA." ["Morning Public Announcement"]. *Chaminade Literary Review* (Spring 1998).

Shadow Dancing:

$elling $urvival in China

Kathryn Waddell Takara, PhD

Edited by Mera Moore

Pacific Raven Press

Ka`a`awa, Hawai`i

http://pacificravenpress.co

© 2017 by Kathryn Waddell Takara, Pacific Raven Press, LLC

All rights reserved. This book may not be reproduced, in whole or in part, including illustrations, in any form (beyond that copying permitted by Sections 107 and 108 of the U.S. Copyright Law and except by reviewers for the public press), without written permission from the publisher.

Pacific Raven Press, LLC
Ka`a`awa, Hawai`i 96730

ISBN: 978-0-9860755-5-1

Cover design and concept by Kathryn Waddell Takara and Nancy Jones Karp

Back cover photograph by Kathryn Waddell Takara

Photography by Kathryn Waddell Takara, and illustration design by Katherine Orr

Book layout by Jonathan Zane, Eien Design www.eiendesignstudio.com

Editing by Mera Moore

This work is licensed under Pacific Raven Press, LLC.

Library of Congress Cataloging-in-Publication Data is available upon request.

Printed in the United States of America

Pacific Raven Press, LLC, is an independent publisher.
http://pacificravenpress.co/
pacificravenpress@yahoo.com

DEDICATION

To my family and to my friends in China

For global understanding, compassion, and hope

TABLE OF CONTENTS

Other Books and Credits ... iii
Dedication ... vii
Table of Contents ... ix
List of Illustrations ... xii
Acknowledgements ... xiii
Introduction ... xv

I   MAGENTA MOMENTS: Teas and Tasty Delights ... 1

Blue Moon in Rising China ... 3
Muted Lakeside ... 4
No Stranger ... 6
Qi Dong Lu ... 9
Sipping Beer ... 10
Father Chef Artist ... 11
Mother Leader Friend ... 13
The Video Man ... 14
Jostling Marketplace ... 16
Favorite Foods ... 18
Aesthetic of Tea ... 20
The Butcher ... 23
The Evening Street ... 25
Home (*wo de jia*) ... 27
Language Is We ... 29
Huadong Winery ... 30
Playtime ... 31
Good Friends and Peony Memories ... 33
Old Performers in the Morning ... 34
Phoenix in Flight ... 35
Riddles ... 36
Monsoon Dinner and Business ... 37

II   TRAVEL GUANXI: Trans-cultural Explorations ... 39

Road to the Great Wall at *Badaling* ... 41
Hidden Gardens ... 43
Chengyang Park ... 45
City Walls and Quiet Remnants ... 47

Train Station	48
The Train	49
Leaving *Beijing*	50
Train Culture	52
Triptychs	53
The Hard Sleeper	54
Jinan Sprawl and Sparkle	56
Blossoming Beauty	51
51 *Dong Hai* Road	57
Badaguan Neighborhood	58
Skygate: *Mount Lao*	59
Shrouded in Silence	61
Apricot Picking	63
The New *Daxue*	65
Lancun	68
Golfing at *Jimo* on Saturday	69
Visiting *Hangzhou*	71
Hangzhou Lullaby	72
All Because of a Cigarette	73

III   MAZE HAZE GAZE: A Rush to the Top   77

Standing Out While in China	79
Under *Beijing* Skies	81
The Double Glory Pavilion and the Communist Party	82
Morning Public Announcement	84
Strength in a Gray City	88
$elling $urvival	89
Hot Like a *Wok*!	90
Towering *Beijing* Cranes	91
Architecture Extravaganza	93
Masters of Allurement	95
Modernization Projects	96
The Art of Survival	98
Power and Prestige	99
Industrial Zones	100
Red Flags	101
China's Food Supply	102
Executive Office	103
Jingcha: The Policeman	104
Beware the Flash	105
Where Were You Last Night?	106
Saturn with a Red Scarf	108

IV	**VEILED TIME: Visions, Spirits, Loss**	**109**

Another Language	111
Dragonflies	112
Mystical *Pagoda*	114
Seasonal Resonance	115
A Day	117
Not Enough Time	118
Longtan Lake Park	119
Oracle Bones and the 1998 *Taiwan* Earthquake	120
Deleterious Time	126
Close Quarters	127
Yearning for Sally's Gifts	128
Disappearances	144
Painful Separation	145
Heat Wave at Midnight	146

V	**OPAL MOON SHADOWS: Lotus Traditions and Generations**	**147**

Bell Culture	149
Gates of China	151
At the Pearl Moon Pavilion	153
The *Great Wall*	155
Retreat at the *Summer Palace*	157
Imperial Steps and Stones	159
At *Qufu*, Home of *Confucius*	162
Revelation at *Mount Tai*	163
Beida (*Peking University*)	164
Stillness and Movement	165
Hidden Splendor	167
Fragrance in Moonlight	168
Stymied in Sunlight	169
Yu Garden	170
Festival of Lanterns	171
Tea, *Taiji*, and Tradition	173
Knowledge for Millennia	177

Glossary	**179**
About the Author	**205**

List of Illustrations

Illustration 1, Author Teaching in *Beijing* and *Qingdao*	xvi
Illustration 2, Author with African Students in *Beijing* and *Tianjin*	xviii
Illustration 3, Chinese Opera in a Red Motif	5
Illustration 4, Author on *Qi Dong Lu* and a Garden with Bottles	8
Illustration 5, Author and Friends	12
Illustration 6, *Qingdao* Marketplace	15
Illustration 7, Favorite Foods	17
Illustration 8, Tea Shop, Tea Bushes, Tea Master	19
Illustration 9, Chinese Opera Performers	24
Illustration 10, Sally's House	26
Illustration 11, Celebrating with Friends at Restaurants	32
Illustration 12, Good Friends and the *Beijing* Subway	44
Illustration 13, Author on Shopping Trip by *Pedicab*	46
Illustration 14, Author Traveling on Trains	51
Illustration 15, Gardener and View of *Mount Lao*	60
Illustration 16, Picking and Selling Apricots	62
Illustration 17, Countryside Area of *Laoshan* District	67
Illustration 18, Author before Moongate; Entrance to a *Hutong*	80
Illustration 19, *Beijing* Street Scenes in 1995	83
Illustration 20, Official Buildings in *Beijing*	87
Illustration 21, Highrises in *Qingdao* and *Beijing*	92
Illustration 22, Traditional Chinese Architecture	94
Illustration 23, Old *Beijing*	97
Illustration 24, Pagoda and Rock Garden in *Qingdao*	113
Illustration 25, Author Wearing *Qipao*	116
Illustration 26, Mists at *Imperial Summer Palace*	125
Illustration 27, Sharing Welcome Teas with Officials	129
Illustration 28, Tea Ceremony at Chinese Opera	131
Illustration 29, Author with Students at University of *Qingdao*	134
Illustration 30, Markets in *Qingdao* and *Beijing*	136
Illustration 31, Author with Officials, a New City Ceremony, and the University	139
Illustration 32, Traditional Chinese Wedding in *Laoshan*	150
Illustration 33, Author Visiting Pavilions in *Beijing*	152
Illustration 34, Author at the *Great Wall of China*	154
Illustration 35, Author at the *Summer Palace* and the *Ming Tombs*	158
Illustration 36, Traditional Chinese Wood Carving	161
Illustration 37, Tea in Village in *Laoshan* District	172
Illustration 38, *Dao* Statues, *Pagoda*, and Temple of *Confucius*	176

ACKNOWLEDGEMENTS

I am so grateful to the following:

The East-West Center for their Asian Studies Development Program (ASDP) to educate and provide travel to American University and Community College professors and administrators in order to responsibly infuse Asian Studies into their curricula;

Elizabeth Buck for encouraging me to apply to the ASDP summer study and travel program to China that was funded by the US Department of Education's Fulbright Study Abroad Program and the Chinese Ministry of Education;
Cynthia Ning and Hao Ping for their skillful and educational leadership on my first trip;

Xue Rong Fang, Guo Cui, Zhang Ming, Philip Sue, Helen Wang, Gu Xiulin and her son Yuan Zhang, Yu Rong Tian and Amigo, and Ma Zi Liang, for their wonderful welcome and friendships including inviting, hosting, making important introductions, housing, and interpreting for me for several summers at Qingdao University, Beijing University of Science and Technology, other universities, and public places to share my research, writing, and knowledge. They invited or accompanied me to dine, lavishly and simply, shop, tour around, and experience daily life on different levels and in various communities in China;

Nancy Jones Karp for her inspiring, creative ideas for the cover and marketing and advertising concepts.

Mera Moore, Karla Brundage, Katherine Orr, Paul Lyons, Manfred Henningsen, Miles Jackson, Allison Francis Payton, Paul Lyons, Elizabeth Buck, and Wu Qing for reading the manuscript in its various stages and for their valuable editorial skills, suggestions, and comments.

Katherine Orr for also helping me with the pictures and their arrangements in Shadow Dancing;

Geriann Almonte and Master Qing Chuan Wang for continuing lessons in taiji and qigong;

Li Ming Tian, Li Xue Hua, Brenda Kwon, Marie Hara, Ishmael Reed, Al Young, Deane Neubauer and many unnamed friends for their music, laughter, company, prayers, visits, support, and encouragement through the years;

Last and first I acknowledge and am grateful for the ongoing loving support and patience of my treasured family who allowed me time to travel, experience, learn, and write.

INTRODUCTION

by Kathryn Waddell Takara, PhD

*If your mind is not clouded by unnecessary things,
this is the best season of your life.* Wumen Huikai (1183-1260)

In ***Shadow Dancing: $elling $urvival in China***, I reflect on ideas about culture, race, identity, and transformation inspired by sojourns in the People's Republic of China. For seven summers (1995, 1998, 2002, 2005, 2006, 2007, 2011), I worked and traveled primarily in Northeast China.

I focus on complex issues ranging across tradition, progress, self-determination, corruption, freedom, individuals, and the state. I explore balance, emulating Chinese culture's traditional advocacy for harmony of *yin* and *yang*. My experiences and observations as a visitor in China challenged me to navigate my identity as a Black woman while simultaneously celebrating Chinese traditions, history, culture, and creativity. For me, personally and professionally, the time spent in China opened another level of self-knowing.

The title aims to capture the veils and shadows of progress, like a *taiji* dancer who watches his or her moving shadow on the ground or wall as the balance changes with each movement into a new space, as well as the relentless push and pull for economic survival, often at a very high cost to both individuals and the state.

My poems bear witness to a society that has been in the midst of tremendous change. I write about the rocketing transformation, from a consciousness of collective national state identity to an expansion of self and the global community, as the Chinese people rush toward individual freedom. I capture moments of drama, humor, and serenity at pavilions, temples, and pagodas, often in the midst of people in movement. I witness the contrasts: old, Soviet-style walk-up apartments and new, luxurious condos and homes; carless streets filled with bicycles and buses, then streets glutted with privately owned cars; stand-up toilets with rough rolls of hot-pink toilet paper, or newspaper, or nothing at all (= bring your own) and comfortable Western-style bathrooms with soft rolls of white toilet tissue and reliable hot water.

As an African American woman visitor, I also examine some history of official attitudes toward Black people in China from the early 20th and nationalist era; China's expansion into Africa during the anti-colonial African independence movements of the 1960s; China's support for the Civil Rights and Black Revolutionary movements including the Black Panther Party in the United States from the 1950s to 1970s; the implementation of and responses to China's African student initiative during the 1980s; and more contemporary connections and opportunities.

I have a particular interest in the China-Africa Education Cooperation policy, which began in 1956 and continues today. Although since the 1949 Liberation, the official policy toward people of African heritage has been that China opposes racial discrimination, many among the Chinese ruling establishment have perpetuated a longstanding tradition of class and color consciousness (not unlike many other cultures) in which those of darker skin—peasants, farmers, and many urban workers—have been considered ignorant and inferior. The carryover of a sense of superiority and entitlement by lighter-complexioned, formally educated persons has introduced a paradox into the policy of encouraging African leaders to educate their brightest youth in China.

While in China, I received enthusiastic welcomes from both authorities and ordinary people, many of whom in the early years had never met or seen an African American. I also experienced sometimes unsettling feelings of acceptable uniqueness. Aside from smiling portraits of African leaders and diplomats with their Chinese counterparts on the walls of government buildings, I witnessed an almost total absence of Black presence in China.

Beginning with my first trip to China from Honolulu in 1995 with an East-West Center group visiting seven universities, I made an effort to connect with African students in China. As a political scientist, I found their presence an anomaly until I learned their history. They were usually participants studying under the China-Africa Education Cooperation Program. In the seven summers, other than students from Africa, I hardly ever saw any Blacks in China, until the last 2 visits when I encountered a few small groups of Black tourists. Most of the African students with whom I talked (the vast majority of whom were young men) complained of poor race relations and institutionalized patterns of discrimination. Many antagonisms they experienced appeared linked to miscommunication and concerns by the Chinese that African men would become romantically involved with Chinese women.

Personally, perhaps because I am a woman, I was not perceived by Chinese men as a competitor for the attentions of Chinese women nor a challenge to their authority. Furthermore, the rocky racial climate in the U.S. may account for the consistently warm reception that I received. Because Chinese schools educate their students about the evils of capitalism and widespread prejudice and discrimination endured by African Americans, I sensed that I was looked on sympathetically. During my visits in the 1990s, Chinese anti-capitalist policies openly supported struggles by Africans American for equality and self-determination. Overall, I was warmly accepted, considered *piaoliang* (pretty, beautiful), found to be exotic and interesting, and respected as a *laoshi* (educated, respected elder). For the Chinese, my status as an American intellectual gave me useful *guanxi* (influential connections). I was seen as having beneficial potential for future projects and joint ventures.

Through the networking of Chinese friends, and, with assistance of interpreters, I delivered lectures at universities in Qingdao and Beijing, including at the National Women's Center in Beijing, offering my unique perspective on struggles for justice in the U.S. I was given the freedom to choose my subjects, including cultural politics, minority literature, gender roles,

problem-solving within and among minority communities, social services, aging, healthcare, and socio-economic benefits and liabilities. In addition, I lectured on Black history and culture and shared my poetry with audiences of Chinese university students, staff, and faculty. My vibrancy in oratory, bold attire and tropical colors, freedom of speech, and fresh intellectual perspectives were appreciated in a society where everyone had been raised to blend in.

For more than 20 years, I have watched China surge to prominence as the world's largest and most industrialized economy. Throughout my visits, I witnessed rapid growth and breathtaking transformation. Recognizing potential, I wanted to invest in or start a joint-venture business, but I lacked know-how, capital, and American business connections (*guanxi*). However, based on my observations and foresight, I shared my vision and enthusiasm to anyone who would listen about the Chinese catapult to power, wealth, and dominance as a result of their dogged efforts and new national slogan and *dazibao*, "To get rich is glorious." Initially, I was deeply impressed by the industriousness of the Chinese people, their thirst and push for knowledge and skills to improve their lifestyles and their nation. I watched as China shifted from a backward economy, changing values and norms to a towering, if uneven, prosperity.

The early inattention of the West to the great waking dragon as it stretched, grew, and thrived was due perhaps to concentrations elsewhere, on various wars, conflicts, and terrorist attacks. From the 1950s through the 1970s, China endured the hidden disasters of Mao Zedong's Great Leap Forward policies, Red Guard, Youth Brigade, and Cultural Revolution. During the 1980s and early 1990s, China still seemed mostly unobserved as it moved toward international competition and prominence through economic expansion, technological advances, development of its space program, and military dominance. Around the turn of the 21st century, even while facing scandals of corruption, poor working conditions, misappropriation of funds, forced abortions, and cyber attacks, the government consistently strove for social stability. As Chinese American author Lisa See aptly observes in her 2003 novel *Dragon Bones*, "The tiger will continue to roar, the phoenix will rise again, but an ant is insignificant." The government has employed such Maoist and Confucian slogans and aphorisms on billboards (*dazibao*), flyers, and posters to unite the country, control the people, disseminate policies, and punish those perceived as disruptive to the national interest.

More recently, China has sanctioned aggressive tactics of global expansion. These include projects in Africa, Southeast Asia, and South and Central America. Notably, China has undertaken massive seabed dredging for land reclamation, turning more than 700 South China Sea reefs into islands, some with landing strips, claiming dominance over the region. Malaysia, the Philippines, and Vietnam view this action as aggressive and threatening. Environmentalists condemn damage to the ecosystem. Western nations perceive a threat to strategic military bases in the Pacific and beyond. However, it should be noted that reclaiming land is not unusual in modern human history: Manhattan and Washington, DC, are both built on reclaimed land, as is Hong Kong. Nevertheless, there is a sense of global urgency about China's economic and military intentions.

Since my first visits in the 1990s, I have witnessed numerous changes in Chinese trade policies; the nation has developed far-flung partnerships and lessened controls over the movements and communications of its huge population. Migrating from rural provinces to the cities in search of work, many thirst for economic security and material well-being. Overturning previous official sanctions such as the 5 Black Categories, the government now permits individual property ownership of property and luxury goods. China has expanded its global presence through banks, property holders, investors, and an increasing U.S. debt to China as Americans buy its inexpensive products. During the past 50 years, China has become a leading world power by encouraging its populace to achieve education, skills, and creativity, especially in science, technology, engineering, and math. Hundreds of thousands of Chinese students have returned from abroad with degrees from Western universities, contributing what they have learned to advance their nation.

Unfortunately, social services and healthcare benefits have become minimal and often inadequate as China transitions from government and family care to privatized, for-profit care accompanied by the break-up and separation of families and communities due to rebuilding, relocating, new cities, and jobs.

The old Confucian principles of authority, obedience, family traditions, and respect (previously condemned as the 4 Olds by the Communist Party) have been modified but remain the philosophical foundation for the Chinese government to control the population through public policies. These same principles have fuelled an astonishing national and international emergence to world status and power. Other vaunted values and virtues of ancient time also continue to persist, sometimes diluted or pushed in the background, both in the government and in the personal lives of families, citizens, and communities. These include respect, honor, modesty, and veneration for elders, ancestors, and Nature. Also prominent in daily life are discipline, protocol, and the values of success, education, reputation, family name and lineage, status and rank, reliability, and beauty/aesthetics. Despite the horrific catastrophes of pollution and other serious environmental challenges that China faces today.

On my visits, whenever I could, I spent time in Nature. I climbed steps at revered mountains like Taishan and Laoshan, walked by lakes and oceans, and wandered in traditional landscaped gardens resplendent with trees, flowers, winding paths, bridges, fountains, and ponds. I felt most comfortable in honored places of relative solitude where I could connect to China's ancient culture, aesthetics, land, and water.

I learned to love the ancient art of brush-and-ink calligraphy paintings displayed in homes, schools, government buildings, and museums, as well as for sale at galleries, shops, and markets. These traditional artworks, created in the past and today by contemporary artists, depict traditional themes of gardens, trees, moon views, and landscapes with mountains, water, and sky—often including tiny human figures, emphasizing the inescapable human presence in the world and the inevitable dwarfing of humanity by the omnipotence of Nature. To the Chinese, their land is a treasure; poets for millennia have written on that relationship.

I was surprised to discover that many superstitions and attempts to connect with the supernatural world persist into the 21st century. There are shamans, wandering mystics, and fortune-tellers, as well as nuns and monks in convents and monasteries. Traces and shadows of Daoism and Buddhism thrive in temples, shrines, pagodas, and even in private homes, below the radar. Buddhist *thangka* painting is appreciated not simply for its beauty but also for its spiritual role. Throngs of Chinese people make offerings and incantations, appealing for protection, looking to remove spells, and seeking to assure good fortune. It remains customary to consult wise women and to turn to astrology and other signs for favorable dates including months and years for cultural rituals such as engagements, weddings, burials, and other occasions and decisions.

Many homes have shrines and altars for ancestors and deities. People make offerings, say mantras, burn incense, visit temples, and keep consecrated objects. They hold ceremonies for purification, absolution, pacification, reverence for ancestral spirits, and initiations, including secular ceremonies. Many ordinary people seek out persons claiming to have magic powers to predict events, give warnings, interpret dreams, endow superhuman strength to individuals to triumph over adversity, and heal by driving evil spirits from the body. Some even believe that blind people connect with unseen energies and are efficacious at healing. Needless to say, the government perceives these persistent superstitious practices as a threat to allegiance and power.

Still, traditional holidays and celebrations continue to thrive and are supported by the government. The lunar New Year, spring festival, lantern festival, dragon boat festival, moon festival, and primal night festival are sanctioned and celebrated with offerings to ancestors, graveside visits, special foods, stories, and entertainment. At these times, charms, incense, amulets, ingots, and herbs are widely available from street vendors and in stores.

In contemporary times, the longstanding philosophical system of *feng shui* has been revisited. Originating more than 3,500 years ago, the system is founded on the principle of harmonization of human life in the surrounding environment. Buildings are constructed to be oriented in auspicious directions of north, south, east, and west, including all of the parts of the buildings: doors, windows, rooms, sitting areas, and placement of furniture such as tables, chairs, desks, and beds. The Chinese affinity for special numbers and myths has also endured. The astrological birth sign is often associated with a number or animal and seen as significant for description of one's personality and for one's future forecast. Likewise, the philosophy of auspicious numbers (4, 5, 8, 9, and 12 are seen to be linked to life's processes and stages, both visible and invisible) has been resurrected from ancient myths, legends, and parables. Numerology frequently appears in cultural references, as with the 3 Friends of Winter, the 3 Plenties, the 4 Gentlemen of Flowers, the 4 Olds, the 5 Black Categories, the 5 Celebrated Fruits, the 5 Blessings, the 8 Treasures, the 8-Spoked Wheel of Law, to mention just a few that are found throughout art, culture, and daily conversation. Chinese people continually employ powerful symbols that relate humans with Nature even as they push forth with science, technology, and official atheism.

By the end of the 20th century, China's leadership was developing international partnerships with other governments and powerful multinational corporations by offering skills, cheap labor, mass manufacturing, and inexpensive goods and services throughout Africa, South America, Southeast Asia, and the Pacific Islands. The Chinese have been successfully trading their expertise in building infrastructure in exchange for the use and often exploitation of other nations' rich natural resources, which China needs for technology, science, and energy.

Today the Chinese government faces a difficult balancing act. On the one hand, it seeks global economic prominence by encouraging opportunities for ordinary citizens (*gongmin*) to travel beyond their provinces for education, jobs, and better lives. On the other hand, when the emigration from rural to urban areas occurs too quickly, the pressures of providing jobs, housing, and other vital services can overwhelm existing resources. As a result, to work in cities, peasants must acquire permits and temporary resident certificates to reside in regulated zones. Sometimes, rural persons ignore these requirements, risking severe punishments in order to earn money to send home to needy families.

Building booms, massive infrastructure projects, growing military might, and newly erected cities have propelled many Chinese industries and corporations to thrive, often at the expense of secure jobs for workers; stable family lives; time-honored traditions and values; old, established urban communities known as *hutong*; and environmental issues. Many of the poor and powerless have been sent to the far west of China to live in unproductive, autonomous, minority zones. Land areas tended by families for generations have been confiscated by the government for "official" projects. In the midst of struggles by the masses to attain middle-class status, material security, survival with dignity, and peace and ease, the government has set the bar to achieving success ever higher. The citizenry have been pushed to learn more, work harder, accept substandard wages, excel in technology, and sacrifice for what is believed to be the greater good.

Management of resources, human rights, food, and health are a conundrum. The government maintains its badge of authority, but recognizes that the population has outgrown the government's capacity to oversee honest functioning in spite of the police, army, commissioners, officials, bureaus, and ministries. Control is also exercised by the media, social networks, and Neighborhood Party Committees whose members (often older women) report on the activities of residents in their assigned areas. There is a well-known saying, "Beat one monkey to frighten the whole pack." Traditional good manners, equilibrium, and modesty are ignored in favor of economic gain and insensitive hierarchies. The practice of integrity and value of equality in the masses has given way to the values of personal gain, the importance of saving face, flattery, and garish materialism.

The message to the world is about China's supremacy. At home, they create gigantic structures, ostensibly to serve the world's largest population. In this push to reach the top, there have been many documented deaths at work sites at home and abroad due to graft and corruption; poor working conditions in mines and factories; and unenforced building standards of schools, housing, bridges, dams, and other infrastructure, some of which have collapsed under natural disasters and pressures to complete jobs quickly.

Corruption by officials in the government and the military and by powerful persons in the business arena includes favors granted in exchange for permits, apartments, and large and small gifts (a tradition dating back to early dynasties). "The fish would die if the ocean were too clean" is an unfortunate popular saying that attempts to justify corruption. The graft has grown out of control at the expense of communities inside China and in other regions where China has influence.

Needless to say, the traditional values of restraint and modesty have fallen by the wayside. Vivid and visible entertainment is encouraged to distract the parts of population who are not immediately involved with national and international conflicts and disasters. Chinese music, operas and other theatrical performances, acrobatics, pageants, singers, dancers, concerts, comedies, and gambling games are common in public halls, parks, squares, market stages, and pavilions. There are also many internet cafes where young people spend hours and days addicted to playing video games thereby missing school and jobs. Places for the public drinking of alcohol, primarily by men, are ubiquitous. Further enhancing their power, status, and finances, the leaders of the New China utilize slogans and symbols to manage the masses in the name of the national good.

China has created the world's most prolific and egregious industry of counterfeit goods and reconstructed parts for sale on street corners and in stores worldwide, especially in Europe, the U.S., and Canada. These goods include pirated American art and music products. The internet has led to a new method for dissemination and delivery of counterfeit products. Fake corporations sell unregulated and sometimes dangerous medications, traditional remedies using body parts from endangered animals such as elephants, rhinos, and tigers, and medical devices, electronics, and technology parts—including mechanical parts sold to the U.S. military, major airlines, car companies, and space industries. This unregulated and often scandalous trade is in addition to the knock-off fashion industry business of fake designer clothing and accessories for export and use at home, sometimes made from dog and cat leather, illegal furs, and unnamed, unregulated, toxic synthetic-blends in plastics, assembled by China's poor, eager, and abundant labor force. Shockingly, China's fraudulent practices have been accomplished with the complicity of American hedge-fund managers, financial planners, realtors, and corporations.

The paradigm of globalism prevails, encouraging production of cheap products, which China produces in bulk due to its massive labor force, despite Western standards of regulation and quality control. For example, some of China's most profitable fraudulent products are pharmaceuticals, especially medications for heart disease, cancer, and other life-threatening ailments. The products are unwittingly prescribed by U.S. doctors, hospitals, and cancer centers.

Most recently revealed is the dangerous boom in trafficking new recreational drugs made in China and sold in the U.S. legally as "bath salts," with names that would appeal to teenagers, such as Bliss, Cloud Nine, and Purple Wave, and wrapped in bright, imaginative packaging. Cheaper, easier to get, and, according to some, more addictive and damaging than methamphetamine and crack cocaine, these drugs, which look like packets of candy, are sold widely in small stores and gas-station marts. They come with a printed warning, "This product is not for human consumption," which protects the sellers. While governments are struggling to eradicate these deadly drugs, many officials in China and in other nations all around the world obfuscate the truth, lie about the products' purposes, and muddy the waters. The leaders of China and other countries would do well to recall a wise Chinese paradigm: "Pride brings loss, humility receives blessings." Some in China and abroad are thriving due to the rapid, cheap production of low cost, unregulated goods and products. Others are dying as a result of those same products.

Another result of greed and growth is the illegal international trafficking of art. Priceless Chinese antiques and national treasures are bought and sold on the lucrative black market and at auctions. They are smuggled out of the country to be placed with private collectors or in museums in the West with false papers to show provenance. A special bureau in China investigates and prosecutes these abuses. An official policy allows offenders to turn themselves in without facing serious penalties—"leniency to those who confess"—but because the problem is so immense the majority of such criminals remain at large.

Chinese expansionism has been especially detrimental to the U.S. manufacturing industry, threatening America's prominence as a world power and trade magnate. New Asian trade accords such as the controversial Pacific Rim Trade Agreement continue to be debated. The Obama administration touts the partnership's benefits to the U.S., but others fear that it will only lead to further disintegration of the American economy.

Larger issues of peace and sustainability have been pushed back in favor of material progress, wealth, and global status. The thoughtful Chinese individual often holds a latent sense of fatalism, evident when faced with national disasters, calamities, and massive death and destruction, while the national collective moves on, often unaware of national and international trends despite smart phones and other digital technology. A level of government censorship and control remain an ongoing obstacle to freedom as defined by American and Western democracy.

In spite of the issues and problems incurred by the Chinese push for world dominance, I have been inspired to create this collection by the warmth and openness of my many Chinese friends. The long history of China's culture and places continually inspires me. I stand in awe of its industrious and courageous citizens' strength, adaptability, flair for style, novelty, and invention, as well as the nation's rich traditions of ritual, protocol, art, and reverence for Nature.

I look forward to a fruitful Chinese future that embraces human rights and peaceful competition. I am optimistic about further balance in international relations and environmental justice. I believe that these advancements will contribute to mutual respect, freedom of choice, greater equality, and world peace.

Shadow Dancing

I
MAGENTA MOMENTS

Teas and Tasty Delights

BLUE MOON IN RISING CHINA

Chrysanthemum emotions hide
complicated secrets in clever corners.

Lights towering above empty skyscrapers
advertise rationalizations of rapid growth.

Hazy full moon struggles to shine through
eerily lit sky tangled with dust and smog.

Fear of specters births inertia
to explore shades of difference.

Bold explorations are trapped
by self-conscious racial difference.

My color stands out
like a ruby persimmon in winter.

The chimerical moon says break free
let go inner considerations.

I welcome smiles and taste new foods
notice flickers and glimmers of familiarity.

Blue moon brews bright confidence
tenders a second chance in this crisp time.

MUTED LAKESIDE

Green superstitions float on this silvered lake.
Powder-blue sky reflects on the ripples.
Men play board games at the edge of wetness.
Women whisper of peace and fidelity in the bamboo grove nearby.

Misty hills, pagodas, mineral pools, and more lakes
Complement quiet voices and the chatter of crickets.
Laughter shatters summer's heavy silence.
July breeze births a joyful holiday.

On rare vacations by the lake, visitors
Share a thermos of plain tea or sip some status scotch.
Air bubbles rise to the water's serene surface.
Big carp hide beneath lilies; a crane observes from pine trees.

Fanciful tales linger on the edges of the trees like specters.
Wrens rest in the willows, then fly away.
Winds stir illicit secrets and dirges drowned in the deep
Muted dramas hidden in the silent testimony of the lake.

NO STRANGER

I

You found me again
a grain of sand
on a beach of becoming.

Amid confusion, pollution, corruption
I sat surrounded by an ocean of tradition
thrilling to warblers singing joy into my heart.

The sea pounded the sand.
Government policies pushed transformation.
People like birds came and went, all strangers.

We 2 survived by oceans of commitment.
I returned once more.
I remember the day when you found me again.

We sat in the sand on an intimate beach.
You beckoned to a passing palmist laden with colorful pearls.
She paused, you bought me a string, and she took my hand.
You translated her lustrous prophecy.

II

Another year found us in front of a university.
I imagined 2 hearts thumping, surprised to find
you patiently awaiting my next visit—you had planned!

You brought me lilies and orchids
an update on national issues
shifting relations and aspirations.

I thought you had lost me.
I am glad you did not.

We met in clandestine intimacy
sat at dusk on the emerald grass
in a shaded grove of sycamore trees
as if bowed in silent prayer
under the early rise of an opal moon near the Pear Tree Pavilion.

Later, a chorus of cicadas
rose and fell like magic charms.
An occasional breeze strummed a melody.
A troupe of willows swayed hypnotically in a graceful dance.

On the watermelon cool night
you spoke of new dangers and held me tight.
Strong and eager as a young warrior
you stayed protectively close by my side
even when I briefly moved and turned.
I felt your close caring, your enthusiasm unbridled.

Bullfrogs and *banqiu* crickets sang our fiery reunion.
Bold stars kissed our skin, no strangers.

Now I have only a melting memory
transparent words in a national aggressive climate of survival
or was it a labyrinth dream, hallucination
of a brilliant reunion and mutinous emotions? No stranger am I. A dreamer yes.

QI DONG LU

In an old tree-lined section
of venerable *Qingdao*
early morning mists greet
residents and visitors alike.

Sturdy stone walls
protect large and substan-
tial homes.
A few people walk early
to the many small markets
buy fried bread
and soy milk
to go with breakfast gruel.

Occasional vendors shout
their services in passing:
Requilting!
Resewing!
Repairing!
Sharpening!
Hauling!

They walk and bike
pulling various carts
their distinctive voices
interrupting respectable
quiet of the neighborhood.

Government and military
get perks in *Shi Dong*
drive big black cars
seatbelts unfastened
speeding chaotically.
In and out of traffic
they race like adolescents
never a ticket, protected
by status license plates.
Taxis, buses, cars jostle
dangerously close
nearly bumping, crashing.

Girls in bright sequined
t-shirts walk arm-in-arm
chattering noisily
stealing glances at the
handsome boys nearby
while waiting for buses
to school and to work.

Near a church
on a busy corner
smartly dressed Chinese
walk to and from
work, shopping, selling
eager for social events.

Foreign tourists
visit scenic sites
in shabby shoes and jeans
oblivious to local protocol.

Specialty stores open
slowly from 8 to 9 a.m.
Along narrow streets
people greet one each
other familiarly at busy in-
tersections on the hillside
overlooking the eastern
shore.

All over the city
business booms
with prestige.
Tall buildings replace
dispensable old *hutong*.
Ordinary *gongmin*
become middle class
almost as quickly as
the friendly wink
you gave to me
on a hot summer day
on *Qi Dong Lu*.

SIPPING BEER

We sat together
At Number 9 *Qi Dong Lu*
Between the old St Michael's Catholic Church
And the 3-story apartment building
In the back garden with the tropical flair
Planted with bright splashes of blue hydrangeas and plate-sized pink roses
Next to the tea plant, bamboo, and the small, white, arched bridge
Listening to the sounds of thrushes
That perched in the tall gingko tree towering above the belfry next door
We sat together for six summers as China expanded to surplus
Sipping beer, eating seafood, savoring friendship.

The trees of *Qingdao* provided cozy nests for birds
Even plum trees for the phoenix that never comes
Offering hope, beauty, and shade for the people.

The choir's practice on the other side of the *Guan Yin* wall
Competed with the *qin* zither practice by my friends' daughter
While church bells announced the hour
And a ghostly fog horn echoed from the harbor.

We sat together
As tourists took quick trips to and from *Golden Beach* on the hydrofoil
Following the national directive to push forward to the top.

Today, 15 years from the beginning
I learn of the divorce, the house no longer a home
Sold to an enterprising young family
My companions scattered, connections shattered
No more sipping beer at *Qi Dong Lu*.
The mother's remarried and living in Denmark.
The father's working in a restaurant and living with relations.
Family life and traditions have been displaced.
I witness dubious patterns of progress and destruction in the New China.

FATHER CHEF ARTIST

Each day, he goes shopping
Between the matches of the World Cup
Football at its finest
Live from 11 p.m. until 5 a.m. in China.
After peeling 100 cloves of garlic
He snatches a nap
Then wakes and chops, chops, chops
fresh food: vegetables, meats, and herbs.

Across the carp pond
Over the small dragon bridge
Beyond the tea plants
He has painted the garden walls for the children
Full of Chinese calligraphy:
Fish, dog, lake, river, family, obedience, success.
In the small east corner of the courtyard
Behind the clothesline on the back wall
He has painted 5 huge circles for the adults
Rings for the upcoming Olympic Games to be held in China.

He regularly accompanies the children
After school to soccer practice, to calligraphy and *qin* lessons
While the mother runs her own small tour company.

Late afternoon, he cooks in the kitchen
Shows the children how to prepare the food
A metaphor for life that lies ahead.
They help with the final chopping to orchestrate dinner.
They stay close to the good smells
Fast-flavored, fried, and boiled dishes.
Chop, chop, chop continues.

For those wiser ones
Who know what twists and turns life can take?
Survival can be surer
If one teaches the children to properly prepare good food.

The father loves family
Will give all his help to true friends.
The man has a good soul
A generous spirit, a sometimes tender heart.

MOTHER LEADER FRIEND

Wang Hua Feng
Organized like a puzzle
The clients, the children
The clothes, the cleaning
Sometimes, the calligraphy, the music classes
Always on the go.

She flows like a river
Between the 4 seasons
Soft as the spring
Burning like summer
Full like the harvest
Brittle and cold to her husband like winter.

Hua Feng helps those who need her
Strives with a smile
Tired but fiery
Sleeps all alone
Dreaming prosperity.

She teaches the children
Leaves cooking alone
Loves to host parties
But does not indulge.

On Father's Day
She makes games with the youngsters.
Charades and poems make all laugh.
For the dads they paint the t-shirts
That Hua Feng lovingly bought.

Hong Mei cigarette smoke all around her
Conjuring the spirits flowing freely.
She emerges a queen.

THE VIDEO MAN

Jack Jiang, the video man
Enters 51 *Qi Dong Lu* early and eagerly
Scans the scene quietly
Sets up his camera
Carefully choosing
Possible backgrounds
Considers shadows and light
As a crane might before a long flight.

He greets the guests kindly
Jokes with the children
Chats, eats spiced dishes, and drinks copiously with the grown-ups
Choosing to make all comfortable.

Jack Jiang, the video man
Grabs his fancy new camera
Slides and glides
Smooth as the *Yangtze*.
Everywhere present he works
Hardly noticed behind the lens of his camera
Invisible to most of the guests at the party
Thrown in honor of the Black American
The *hei meiguaren*, and the 4th of July.

The consummate professional
Who pretends to be a jester
Jaunty and confident with his heart of gold
The video man works wonders
With creative eyes
Sensitive imagination
Sturdy hands and his true camera.
A product sure!

JOSTLING MARKETPLACE

A day of blues and grays
Clouds and fog like curtains
The sun on stage, then hidden
Exploring, touring, and discovering surprise gifts
We part for a while, do our separate work.
At nightfall we go out to shop
Jostle through the open marketplace
Select sweet fruits and flowers
Peruse endless-seeming tables and buckets of fish and crustaceans
Baskets and cages of birds and small animals.
We squeeze through 1,000s of local Chinese shoppers.
The market is teeming with voices, vendors, fresh living food
Scores of unfamiliar sounds, people, and smells
Enticing traditions enduring.

FAVORITE FOODS

I sit in the land of *Kongzi, Confucius*
enjoy the daily banquet of spectacular fare
each delicious preparation
a mouthful and ocean removed from home:
1,000 preparations
hot pots, steam boats
Beijing duck
sweet and sour pork
tripe, liver, and kidney BBQ on a stick
unforgettable dumplings
endless varieties of turtle, snails, and other soup concoctions.

What will I miss the most?

At regular banquets, ever the guest of honor
I sit in a special chair facing the entrance in the north seat
for a 9-course meal
or a 15-course meal
or a 21-course meal!
The water is non-potable, so it is hot tea to drink
or bottled soda or beer, or very exceptional imported wine.

Even the appetizers are rare:
paté, peanuts, seeds, seaweed, clams, garlic, ginger, and pickled delights.

Dinner is mixed plates:
Lu cuisine, numerous preparations
various sauces, vegetables, noodles
lotus roots, chicken, duck, horse
snake, frogs, slugs, scorpions
soups, eggplant, spinach, and greens
red fish, river fish
jelly fish, cuttle fish
dried fish, prepared fish, fresh raw fish
clams and oysters
shrimp and conch
seaweed and mushrooms
fungus and peanuts
hot, boiled, fried, baked, and steamed
and rice at the end of each meal for a filler
followed by completion with daily watermelon
which not unlike tea
cleanses the palate, aids in digestion, and relaxes the body and soul.

AESTHETIC OF TEA

He cha? Would you like some tea?

Upon a tour of the tea museum in *Hangzhou*
I tasted and learned of a magnificent cosmos of teas.
Thousands of years ago in diverse districts and provinces
Laoshan, Sichuan, Yunnan, Hangzhou, Guizhou
great tea growers and trees towered like kings and dragons.
Teas reached renowned status including special teas only for royalty.
Different teas had properties of *yin* or *yang*.
Tea fragrances were discovered and developed: *lychee*, jasmine, *puerh*.

Ceremonies developed based on tea services
for Imperial families, holidays, rituals
spread by literati and nobles in yellow silks.
An aesthetic culture emerged as tea was sipped by the leisured ones
on sitting stones in elaborately designed gardens beside manmade ponds
while meditating, conversing, painting near stands of willow trees
or in the shadows of carved eaves of a Pavilion of Green Delights.

Tea themes with scholars thrived in conversation
or in artistic meditation painted on porcelain
or on silk screens featuring mountains, gardens, pavilions
yellow hibiscus, purple irises, red camellias, ornate sculptural rocks, butterflies
small men against a backdrop of a few familiar trees
overshadowed by the large dance of Nature.

Classical Chinese poets of the *dao* like *Lu Yu* and *Yu Men*
and modern tea masters like *Popchong Sunim* and *Ni Hua Ching*
advanced the study of tea and the tea philosophy known as *Way of Tea*.
Philosopher *Li Shizhen* even wrote a compendium on teas and health.
Many scholars composed innumerable tea classics in novels and poems.

Particular tea preparations became famous and refined
the place and timing of the harvest significant
the processes of drying by wind, sun, or fire recorded.
Methods of stringing and hanging developed, away from odors
for optimum storage: warm/dry/fresh air.
Recipes developed for pressed, spread, cooled, and fried tea leaves.
Brewing by steeping became the best and most favored!

He cha? Good tea brings good health.

Innuendoes of color convinced the rulers, royalty, and literati of lineages of tea
its valuable property of long-life preservation.
The leisured cultivated a palate to discern the quality
the ease to drink, the need for good pure water
from rain water/snow water/waterfalls/mountain streams.

Artists were commissioned by royalty and high officials
for the parallel creation of various elegant and unique utensils
precious porcelain and ceramic pots, cups, covers
tiny woven baskets, strainers, wooden spoons, grabbers, and more
using assorted visual media, colors, and shapes
to enhance the experience made for special occasions, purposes, and teas.

Chefs created tea cakes and biscuits for the leisured ones.
Healers discovered 15 minerals in tea.
Certain harvest months and places related to the cure of maladies were favored.

He cha?

Nowadays, scientists and nutritionists examine the harvest
prepare over 500 organic compounds for tea remedies.
Special teas bring solutions to health
stimulate digestion
promote calmness and sleep
aid in weight loss and reduce cholesterol
help relaxation, boost the immune system, ease bleeding
sooth bites and sunburns.

Other teas, sometimes bitter
help eject phlegm, cleanse the urine and eyes, ward off colds
offer relief from hiccups, hangovers, stress, and colic
increase the milk flow in nursing mothers
eliminate grease from the inner body-country
lower our internal heat for good elimination, bring earth to the healing.

A few rare teas are said to cultivate our spiritual being
activate the *lian dan shu*, our energy center.

Everywhere green tea is considered good tea culture
praised for creating a healthy immune system and long life.
Oolong, fennel, lavender, green butter tea—all promise a mend.
Special varieties of tea are found propitious for the heart or kidneys.
Tea as an anti-cancer agent, and even chemotherapy!
Tea as a natural stimulant reputed to enhance sexuality!

He cha?

After our tour of the tea museum
we stopped and rested near the Mists of Remembrance Pavilion.
Fields of tea bushes swayed gentle undulations
and some strains of *Hangzhou* tea branches were dark like my skin.

We changed clothes at the steaming Olympic mineral pool
swam, lounged in pool chairs, drank scotch
while white butterflies danced on the fruit trees nearby.
During a stolen moment in the water
you touched me and looked into my eyes.

I imagined another lifetime 100s of years ago
we in silk robes and stunning jade ornaments
hidden in a garden near a tea bush field
over the hillock and white arched dragon bridge
we behind the rounded scholar's rock inscribed with a painted poem in red calligraphy
sipping hot tea perfectly brewed
by the nearby bamboo stand of tensile strength
we whispering poems, touching hands, and aware of new encircling conditions
biting tongues between tasting tea
sharing smiles under sizzling blue skies and verdant earth
unruffled by perennially turbulent times.

He cha?

THE BUTCHER

In the kitchen, the butcher waits
just beyond the reach
of the dragon oven's protective fire.
He waits until the customers arrive
to demonstrate his artistry.

Zhuangzi said, "Let the joy of the keen blade work."
Again and again
the butcher carefully finds the space between the joints
each animal an opportunity to demonstrate his skills.
He cuts the carcasses of chicken, pig, lamb, goat, and cow
sometimes horse, buffalo, whale, bear, deer, and even cat or dog.
When the parts fall away, clean as a warm breeze, he cleans his blade.

He is a symbol of how to live a life through observations and skill.
Is there a norm of good and right?

THE EVENING STREET

After work at dusk
millions of bodies
ordinary citizens
move and surge like a swollen river.
Along the city streets
people ebb and flow
past the 100,000 street vendors.
Some stop to buy, to bargain, to bet
to cut hair, sharpen scissors.
Others visit the specialty shops
practice *taiji* and Western-style ballroom dancing
incongruous in the crowded neighborhood squares
oblivious of trouble and betrayal.

Merchants display their wares on ample well-lit sidewalks
or on dark side streets and alleyways for the more transitory sellers
of crafts, recycled goods, and cheap knock-offs of fancy brands
all eager for business.

Young women sparkle sophistication
adorned with shiny beads, sequins, and rhinestones
fashionable pants and sparkling shirts
summer silk dresses and high-heeled leather shoes.
Parading along the walkways, seeking smart buys and attention
arm-in-arm they walk and talk
slowly passing the shops and stores above and below street level.

Men of all ages look casual in jeans or slacks, neutral colors
occasionally shirtless if the heat is extreme
chat with friends, cough and spit.
Some walk miniature dogs.
Groups play checkers, cards, and *mahjong*
on portable plyboard tables and small folding stools
while still others gather and watch a game of sports on TV.
Often the men will stop at the shirtless bawdy vendors
of famous fresh *Qingdao* draft beer
and while away the evening until 9:30 or 10:00
when they amble home, according to curfew, and turn in.

HOME (*WO DE JIA*)

Mornings I sit in my space on the 3rd floor of the penthouse
inhaling a soporific breeze of incense bought at the temple
where I offered a sweet bundle for the ancestors
and gratitude for pluperfect moments.

Oh Grandma Tai Tai calls to me from downstairs, "*Nihao!*"
I pretend to be sleeping and not hear her summons.

I rejoice to be inspired to write a poem for old friends
who recently escorted me to the seashore
to recover from travel and renew memories
where they hosted me to long, luxurious *yin-yang* banquets
sharing endless dishes of Shandong delicacies
jiaoze, noodles, and *les fruits de mer*
shrimp, crayfish, clams, oysters, jellyfish, and mullet
unknown bugs and insects
and endless varieties of seaweed
Tsingtao beers by the dozen
between toasts, cheers, eating, and storytelling
topped off at the end by assorted melons, other fresh fruits
lychee dessert reminding me of the words of *Su Dongpo*.

I feel cared for in this faraway land.
The people are warm and welcoming
willing, patient, and hardworking.
In my solitude, I am grateful for the gift of friendship.
While I write in the mornings, I drink tea, ritually brewed.

Predictably I am interrupted.
Grandma *Tai Tai* calls to me yet again.
"*Nihao. Chi guo fan le ma? Nihao!*"
I reluctantly descend the too-steep stairs from my 3rd-floor flat
repeat that I am not hungry, *bu yao chi fan.*
But she pretends to not understand my Chinese
does not accept my impolite response.
"*Jiali,*" she says, be at home.

She has cooked again and wants me to taste
Chinese fried crullers
jiaoze dumplings
and her special congee with pickled turnips, salt eggs, and dried dates.
She does not want me to cook my grits
carried all the way from *Hawai`i*.
She does not want to eat them either.

She waits patiently for me at the bottom of the stairs, bent in half but mobile.
Her back is parallel to the ceiling, a toothless smile lighting her face and eyes.
No longer surprised by my foreignness she does not judge me by my color.
I am not *yang quizi*: a white devil, rich, spoiled, decadent.
I am not a CEO or investor, but a respectable *jiaoshi*
a professor to be served and honored for my education.
I am an esteemed Other.

Grandma Tai Tai persuasively offers me other leftovers
spicy shrimp and tangy cooked cucumbers
warmed-over liver and steamed ginger fish
greens and mushrooms
brought home last night
from a banquet at a nearby *fandian*
and of course her delicious *jiaoze*.
How can I refuse such tasty delights?

Nonetheless, I also fry 3 eggs
get a roll of *mianbao*
and try to taste everything! Her foods and mine.

Grandma *Tai Tai* sits with me
breaks the silence and says something I do not understand.
"*Jiali*," she repeats.
I remember the meaning: home, beauty, a girl's name.
She has given me a name, "Good and beautiful."

Later, I shower.
She says, "*xixi*," wash up, wash up.
I ponder our out-of-pattern morning together
and slowly recognize
she is teaching me. Family. *Jiating*.

LANGUAGE IS WE

Language
a magic wand can
transform a life
transmit a history
preserve a culture
develop concepts.

Language a golden key
can open doors
give opportunities
teach new knowledge.

Language
a secret symbol can
accessibilize people and things
convey comforts
create profits.

Language
a human tool can
reflect nature's laws
perpetuate abstractions
create metaphors, symbols, and myths.

Language
a window can
teach values and principles
gather families and friends
transform me and I to us and we.

Mandarin, calligraphy, *pinyin*
symbols on dragon bones 5,000 years old
how can I learn quickly the language?
Me at over 50? I can, I will, continue . . .
I listen to the language of eyes and hearts.

HUADONG WINERY

A rare bottle of chardonnay.
A vanguard European-style winery.
A new social climate of openness.
What are such privileges
Without good friends?

A busload of chattering *waiguo* academics and our Chinese escorts
Lurch along a precarious narrow hot dirt road in a honking bus.
"Countryside *Hua Dong* Tours" offers visitors fine wines and varietals
Plates of ripe fruits that inspire loose conversations and high spirits.

Guides, leaders, functionaries, and guests enjoy
The bright noon break
A few glasses of fine clear wine
Delicious offerings of *gala* and *les fruits de mer* in a scenic landscape
And pots of fresh-brewed tea throughout the afternoon.

Serious later, still carrying a wine buzz
I remembered seeing the scowls of workers
laboring under the blazing summer sun in the winery's vineyard.

PLAYTIME

Peaches and plums
affluence, abundance, fragrant consciousness.

A veil of seduction
plays between Jade Mountain, the sea
and the fishing villages and towns all around.

Like children
you and I play hide and seek
in a coastal city in *Shandong* Province.

Unlike children we stumble uncontrolled
Un-self-consciously.

GOOD FRIENDS AND PEONY MEMORIES

After
duck dumplings and *congee*
morning rush and stuffed buses
acupuncture and a massage
in the old section near *Longtan* Lake Park

After
classes, computer time, meetings
email and office work
editing a short ghost story
and a long sweaty walk going to market

After
a green bottle of *Tsingdao* beer
Chinese dinner with grits added from America
watermelon, peaches, dried figs
and a porcelain vase of red and purple peonies on a rosewood table

After
loud thunder and torrential showers
iron pots and dishes washed
and hearing through the traditional grapevine
about flooding, drownings, and great destruction down South
the national call for army recruits to report for dangerous rescue efforts

After the state news on *CCTV*
and a few belches of contentment . . .

We smile and share
friendship, warmth, and delight
word pictures of our day.

Then you leave me
alone with compassionate *Guan Yin*
incense burning in opal moon tranquility.

After a steaming cleansing shower
I feel happy, soft, and secure in our friendship.
Just before lights out in a nighttime of purple fatigue
I anticipate magenta peony dreams.

OLD PERFORMERS IN THE MORNING

The Cyprus Garden at the *Temple of Heaven*
Provides a space
For old men and women
To relive their past splendor
Practice the *qin*
Sing the old *Beijing* operas
With enthusiasm
Projecting their voices above
The loud groups of *erhu* players.
The singers lift their chests
Puff out their trim body frames and lean forward
Complete with classical hand motions.
Some of the ladies wear gloves.
The men have large fans
As props for their romantic pasts and familiar roles.

PHOENIX IN FLIGHT

A day in and out, motion and stillness
visiting the Buddhist temple and parks
a peace is discovered in the courtyard
under the leaning, wandering pines
symbolizing longevity and venerability.
3 small cones brought home
reminded me of *Tao Yuanming*.

Exploring and shopping
new spaces and emotions
sensing different textures
in on-shore breezes, this was
a *phoenix* day full of promises
intimations of discovery and
unspoken dreams.

We built a monument of friendship
a new dance to the ebb and flow
of modernization and mutable moods
observed growing unemployment visible
mammoth new buildings with
empty windows looking out to the sea
waiting for future inhabitants
worried bankers facing
international competition
and looming Asian economic crisis.

We feigned indifference
to the unseen forces
tried to communicate
across cultures, beyond tongues
in a silence of togetherness
discerning the smallest gestures
to better understand
the patterns of attraction
moments shared.

We searched for a link
to make a deeper connection
to ask the right questions
to listen to the answers
in music and brassy green noise
in awkward forbidden steps
not daring to whisper
our red dreams
trying to understand the emotions.

The rains came and went
like thunder, like lives, like we did
from place to place
wanting to play freely
like children
trying to act responsibly
like adults
eating clams and shrimp
drinking tea, beer, and wine
somehow incomplete.

Finally before moonrise
tired but happy as the sun-filled day
I left you to return home and eat *jiaozi*
burn sandalwood incense
in the shiny brass burner
engraved with a dragon and *phoenix*
bought at the temple
along with the prayer beads
ever grateful
for the breath of Nature
the 4 directions
the sacred smoke
beautiful *Guan Yin* moments
in a context of compassion in flight.

RIDDLES

I
Why try to stay and succeed
when we see ourselves like water
fade into a mere trace of infinite and unfamiliar space
shimmering drops on a dim, uncharted path?
Why try again?

II
But for those we love
is it enough to try to capture
that fleeting pseudo-sensation of joy
that unutterable hope
of another tomorrow?
A promise of tradition. We try again.

III
I sent you away
you of whom I dreamed.
I could not face an unknown future
with or without you.

I closed my jade door
when I wanted your gossamer gift of love
the taste of my imminent absence
obscured by our green present.

IV
I ignored your calling
even as I fought my moon-struck feelings.
I wanted to hold and be held by you.

My veil of illusion
fluttered between heaven and earth
obscuring the portal to the iridescent pool of presence.

V
I feared the shadowed specter of solitude
behind my opalesque door of hope
bamboozled with and without you.

MONSOON DINNER AND BUSINESS

My last night in *Qingdao*, I met your family
In the neighborhood of *Dong Hai* at a fancy restaurant that seats 1,000
the giant first floor ringed in 100s of large- and medium-sized aquariums
with every imaginable fresh fish
and small live edibles like snakes, frogs, and snails.
Who knows what the kitchen held in cages for intimates
in this *hen gui*, very expensive, exclusive place?
My hot pink flowered dress drew attention.

In a private room you placed me facing the southern entrance
with the other guests of honor around me.
We talked import-export with no resolution or contracts to sign.
In good faith we sealed a joint partnership
with plenty of promises and *ganbei* toasts to assure follow-up.
You and your family ordered 12 dishes and we drank 12 quarts of beer
At least 6 for good fortune on my imminent *bon voyage*.

By the end of the evening, we were all laughing, slightly tipsy
feeling like family.
You accompanied me as I set out for the dark walk
to my penthouse up the hill
sloshing along in the arriving deluge.

The streets were quickly becoming deserted
not crowded like the day we snuck down alleys
meeting illegal dealers in antiquities
to see and perhaps purchase a few forbidden national treasures
daily for sale on the underground market.

Hardly a soul out on the street at 9:30 p.m.
my skimpy silk *qipao* dress and new beige leather shoes
were quickly soaked from heavy drizzle and cobblestone walkways
with drenching rains and floods from a no-name monsoon
still a day away and moving north, toward us.

We tried hard to squeeze together
under a single umbrella
to avoid the inevitable ending of a time-place relation
laughing too loudly to mask our smoldering emotions
ever mindful of the surprise of yet another *typhoon* in the news
threats of cancelled flights, unknown tomorrows
and gratitude for the whirling memories and unforgettable send-off.

II

TRAVEL GUANXI

Trans-cultural Explorations

ROAD TO THE *GREAT WALL* AT *BADALING*

On the road to *Badaling*
rain fell while spirits roared
we in bus limbo
bouncing between destinations
beyond the hordes of *gongmin* riding on endless bikes
through strands of towering apartments and new *fanze* homes
to and from urbanization and suburbs
across wheat fields and peach orchards
toward fulfillment of another cymbidium dream.

On the road to *Badaling*
we practiced counting in Chinese
saw pearl opalescence rising across the hazy sky
to complement the colorless day
wondering what was to come
through the fogs of calligraphy and foreign tongue
across the plains of otherness.

On the road to *Badaling*
on the watermelon cool day
conversation darted like swallows
until we stopped and ate fresh peaches in the rain
under our varicolored umbrellas.

During our 7-story descent to the marble burial chambers
we followed our guides to explore the royal *Ming Tombs*
moved mechanically with the throngs—wet, sweaty, steamy
who tossed coins into the narrow void, offerings to antiquity.
We passed through the stifling underground tunnel
then quickly emerged from the vault of *Dingling* and *Tomb of Stability*.

Back on the road to *Badaling*
we stopped once more to walk the Sacred Road
bordered by humongous pairs of marble statues
mythical giants with massive hooves and feared teeth
a surreal and silent drama of imagination.

On the road to *Badaling*
silence fell on the group like scattered showers and yellow winds.
Almost imperceptibly, mists appeared
shrouding the wall of 10,000 li in mystery.

As we began our descent to *Jiayuguan* Pass, the road to *Badaling* ended abruptly
at a narrow gate where tour buses squeezed through
to discharge the scores of sightseers eager to walk the Wall of Epiphanies.

Following a light meal arranged by our leaders in a small restaurant
we began the arduous climb up along a portion of the *Great Wall of China*
slow and steady—straining, puffing, marveling
silently praying for protection from the ill-maintained high places
giving thanks for spectacular and unpredictable moments in the rising mists of *Badaling*.

HIDDEN GARDENS

Through ornate inner gates
hidden between towering apartment blocks
and new condominiums
tucked in the grassy areas called green space
I see stone tables, stools, small vegetable gardens, and flowers
where urban elders gather daily, play cards and *mahjong*
walk their small well-groomed dogs
sun their caged birds
talk story and gossip about the goings-on in the community
with or without the nosy building super and *Neighborhood Party Committee*.

Corners of hollyhocks, lilies, azaleas, and rosebushes
grow silently next to fragrant herbs and camellias
under tall gray faceless windows.
Morning gardens offer illusion of solitude
for *taiji* practice and dancers' creative camouflage of motion
behind the fir trees and thick morning mist
for early shadow boxing with neighbors or alone
green joy amid the secret silent gnarled stones
patterns arranged by masters and artists.

CHENGYANG PARK

We wanted to watch the full moonrise in Nature
decided to make a picnic in *Chengyang* Park
rode northeast in a lurching taxi
along the 4th ring of the freeway
past the flower-lined parks and gardens
the elegant new townhouses
occasionally bridging over stinking polluted streams.

We arrived at the large park near dusk
walked across the dragon bridge
beyond the yellow rock garden over the grassy knoll
to the larger expanse of water
where ducks swam in wedges
toward their evening cove of rest.

We carried our picnic sacks filled with *jiaozi*
previously rolled, stuffed, and boiled in the early afternoon.
Fresh summer fruits and tepid *Laoshan* beer made our load heavy.
Our hearts danced light like jazz as we searched for the perfect place to sit.

We took pictures with cameras, cell phones, and memories
ate and watched the sunset reflecting golden splashes across the lake
that accentuated the gaily painted red, blue, and green pavilion
with gilded pillars and fluted edges
while happy children learned to roller-skate in the rink nearby.

Without warning, clouds gathered near the darkening horizon.
Lightning flashed menacing the hot summer evening electric.
Portending rain felt dangerous like red thunder in turgid air.
Throngs of people suddenly scurried toward home in the unforeseen chill.

Across the gilded lake, a woman steadily sang
freely practicing Chinese opera
her voice strong and clear as a temple bell
ringing sound melodies
undeterred by the competition of urban noise and impending deluge.

In the distance, towering over a slice of lingering rosy skyline
an impressionable sketch of irregular modernity
a giant crane still worked, lifting, moving tons of materials:
24-hour shifts steady as each passing hour
completion deadlines hovering on a moment's shoulder
before the *Beijing* Olympic Games in 2008!

CITY WALLS AND QUIET REMNANTS

Ample flower boxes line the 5-ring freeways
Surrounding *Beijing* beyond the ancient wall of the city.

Nature's colors riot like fireworks
Peonies, marigolds, daisies arranged artistically
Whizzing by at eye level
Along the smoggy, crowded roads.

Non-descript aluminum fencing in new rich communities
Replaces old rock and mud walls, where entrances to *hutong*
Traditionally were guarded by statues of dragons and fearful beasts.

Immense 20-story buildings crowd the skyline
Replace shaded communities and intimate courtyards
With cars parked illegally on sizzling sidewalks
While soon-to-be defunct bicycles and old-fashioned palanquin *pedicabs*
Weave in and out of crowded, continual traffic.

On some few old remaining tree-lined streets
Willow trees, *lotus* ponds, and parks with small pagodas tucked behind walls
Provide shade, rest, and quiet inspiration for the weary population.

At the 4th Ring Road, at least 5 overpasses
Crisscross crazily above each other
At night illuminated by thousands of tiny lights along the modern walls.

Underneath the precarious balance of freeway walls all around
In the almost tree-less part of another new addition to the city
Old Chinese men cluster nightly in circles around small wooden containers
Makeshift tables with game boards and pieces on top.
They sit on squat folding stools with their beer and snacks
Drinking, laughing, cooling off from their sizzling apartments
Gambling on Chinese checkers with their *pengyou*, friends.

A few traditions and remnants of friendships remain amid the changing walls.

TRAIN STATION

Before the late afternoon departure from the *Beijing* train station
We attended an early-morning tea ceremony
An intricate adventure in Tea Town
With 7 different teas, processes, harvests, fragrances
Tiny pots, cups, doused in boiling water
At each different tasting
Various wooden implements and woven-reed sieves.
Tea leaves smelled and tasted like rare French wines.
I am friends with the tea master and calligrapher.
His mirth, sparkling eyes, and dancing spirit
Make one forget the sweltering day.

Afternoon at home
Packing and repacking my bags 4 times for a 2-week journey
We dragged the bags down the 7-story walkup
Hailed a cab and hurried to the train station
In downtown *Beijing*, 105 degrees at rush hour.
A sudden darkening
The sky was ripped by summer lightning.
Thunder growled in the distance.

Evening throngs of Chinese travelers
Crowded the grand plaza in front of the train station
Some waiting, playing cards, chess, go, *mahjong*.
At the entry
Everywhere pushing
        To show the ticket
        To squeeze through the gate
        To pass security
        To climb the stairs
        To wait sweating in line
        To hear the announcements only in Chinese
        To show the ticket
To pass the turnstile
Passengers swarmed the platforms
Frantically searching for their cars
Their seats
Their bunks
The tea thermos
A place to put their baggage.
I was jostled along, anxiously joining the unimaginable masses.

Suddenly the rains poured down in torrents
just as the train pulled out, exactly as scheduled, 8:12 p.m.

THE TRAIN

Hurtling through the Northeast China countryside
On a somber gray day after a big rain
We watch orange tile roofs flash by
Everywhere industry and agriculture.

Hundreds of cranes tower above as we pass villages/towns/cities
Tree farms and orchards of 10,000 plums, peaches, apricots, poplars
       And other unknown tree varieties, thin young trunks supporting heavy spring leaves.

The train speeds past new brick villages, old gray *hutong*
Fresh paint on all public thoroughfares
       Likely to be seen by the foreigners traveling in China.
Spacious fields of brown and green rectangles
       Recline across the flat land as far as the eye can see
Where solitary farmers or small groups
Work large plots bounded by rows of trees
Grow corn, eggplant, beans, melons, asparagus, parsley . . .

We pass small old houses plastered gray over red bricks.
The wheat harvest is over, apricot season in full swing
Some fields burned, fallowed, and ready for the second planting
Rain puddles and yellow wildflowers abound
Ponds and rivers are cleaner than in the previous 12 years
       Of algae, chemical waste, and other debris.

Railroad tracks criss-cross, intersect, or pass over each other
Revealing the complex networks of transportation
And rapidly expanding urban and industrial zones
Across the northeast agricultural belt of the People's Republic of China.

In occasional country graveyards, irregularly spaced tombstones
Awkwardly placed, lean like giant ghosts.

Wet highways, slippery roads, and muddy ponds do not deter the farmers
Who must be happy not to have to carry
Endless buckets of water to moisten each plant.

LEAVING *BEIJING*

Beginning day, heavy, gray, obedience pressing forward for officialdom
neglected dreams stacked tall in the corner, repressed by sanctioned authority
mists of remembrance unveil hope and fear and obligation.

On the way to the stately architectural wonders in the countryside
we pass new buildings bursting forth cement phalluses
in baffling leaps of progress
24-hour shift work, low pay, inadequate housing
short-term permits to stay in the city.

Young farm workers' strong backs break cement streets and roads
using wooden mallets, picks, and determination to escape poverty
despite the impending environmental disaster, ecological genocide
all poised to destroy *lotus* traditions and generations of survival.
The old and the new have become enemies.

TRAIN CULTURE

On the train with white lace curtains
Chinese classical music plays
Before each stop.
The tidy *fuwuyuan* sells ramen packs in bowls
To be heated from the gallon-size hot-water thermos
Found tucked under the table in each car of the hard sleeper.
She has soft drinks, sodas, and sweet snacks.
She calls as she passes, *"Chi fan le ma?"*
Men travel on trains
Eat boiled noodles and snacks
Peanuts and sunflower seedsDrink *pijiou* (beer) and clear white *jiu* (whiskey).
Men move to the open space between the cars
Eager to smoke, laugh, and swear together.
Comrades, mostly men, after eating lunch, take care of each other, forever friends.

TRIPTYCHS

T-26, car 12, seat 26
Bottom row, hard sleeper
6 bunks, large hot-water thermos.

Small table, comfortable clean quilt and pillow
Convenient hook to hang clothes
One can stretch out and take a rest.

Train-tripping is a good way to travel
Daydreaming at the windows
on the high-speed convoy.

White stones and sculpted passages
Etched on the hillside like roman arches
Entertain the passing passengers.

We whiz by vineyards, quarries, large highways
Unnamed trees, mountainous piles of coal
Isolated clusters of hills, *lotus* root farms, great fields of rice paddies.

Thousands of farmers up to their knees in mud
All flash by as I notice my sorry sore ass
Only halfway to *Beijing* and already 5 hours sitting on the train.

Hundreds of nameless trees on spindly trunks
In forest farms stretch to the horizon
Some now taller than telephone poles.

Alone I wonder where you are now
Watching another landscape
Traveling speed to new possibilities, under a fading sun.

Flood waters recede reflecting the early evening moonlight
Adorning rice paddies in a mystical silvery patina
Mirroring jade shadows in a *Du Fu* countryside seen fleeting by from Train 26.

THE HARD SLEEPER

Around *Weifang*
A red sunrise at 5 a.m., the hazy fields are full of dew.
Inside the train, passengers on the hard sleeper still doze.
Outside the passing windows, farmers tend their gardens
Cultivating in the same ancient way to feed the multitudes
With antiquated hoes, scythes, and buckets of water
Carefully distributed by hand around each plant.
They park their old bicycles nearby.
Apricot, cherry, and peach trees border the plots.
A select few favored farmers use hoses and drive tractors.
Factory towns border the seemingly endless fields.

The wheat harvests lie stretched out on seldom-used roads.
Women bend low, threshing with whisks and brooms
Separating the chaff
Grateful for dry days before the portending rainy season
Oblivious to the passing train.

Tall chimneys spew black smoke
From nearby coal power plants, thriving industries.
Countless new apartment blocks
Surge like tall gray ghosts
House the flood of migrant workers
The displaced dwellers of ancient *hutong* in distant cities.

The train moves slowly across *Shandong* Province
Over newly constructed tracks
Over rough cement ties
Past endless piles of coal and cement rubble
Past the race of modernization.
The engineer skillfully avoids abandoned routes and old tracks.

Passengers awaken to the jerks, lunges, and thuds
Cough, spit, call on cell phones, talk to friends and loved ones
Walk up and down the aisle of the hard sleeper on the way to their destinations.

JINAN SPRAWL AND SPARKLE

Half the distance
Between *Qingdao* and *Beijing*
Sprawls *Jinan*, ancient capital of *Shandong* Province
The train takes only 10 minutes on the middle fast track to go in and out of town
Small miracle, considering the traffic of millions.

Too hot in summer, too cold and drab in winter
Jinan is full of government functionaries
A meeting place of high party officials, like mayors and governors
Ready to delude the masses for promotions and progress.
Jinan stands firm under the red thumb of *Beijing*
Housing countless bored prisoners and fear-filled dissidents.

The train slows.
Look! On the fleeting sidewalks, artistic and flashy barrettes, belts, and shoes
Brightly colored clothes move
      Every way different
      Tradition and vanguard.
Everyone must be unique and sparkle.

After *Jinan*, next stop *Tianjin*.
We spent 2 days and toured the city, a temple, factories.
At the university, I met students from Kenya, Nigeria, and Uganda.
We discussed race and class and took pictures together, the *Afro-diaspora*.

BLOSSOMING BEAUTY

Lovely amber roofs and cypress trees parasol the inhabitants and visitors
all delighting in the abundant seafood and treasured fruits.

In the mornings, residents invite me to local parks
for *taiji* and *qigong*, which offer balance and energy and friendship.

Qingdao seems like a single flower on a misty hillside,
timid in the bustling yellow dawn of emerging deafening growth.

The city's history of industriousness and multiculturalism
mirrors in the residents' diligent eyes and cheerful smiles.

Narrow streets are lined with poplars and Chinese conifers
Gardens replete with pink roses, red peonies, and lavender hollyhocks.

The mountains' serenity around the city contrasts with the urban crescendos
life advancing like rapid brooks into reservoirs of pollution and prosperity.

In the golden sun, children flutter like bright butterflies
their colorful kites dancing on the flowing wind currents.

Many kind hosts prepare and share exquisite marine cuisine:
scallops, sea cucumbers, prawns, red porgy, and rare conch.

In the indigo evening, the sea soothes the city with a gentle lullaby
and ocean breezes dance through the gardens and rooms of contentment.

The opal moon is only half full on the night of our departure
as if signaling regret for the sad separation of new friends.

Yes, we will never forget the smiles and blossoming beauty of *Qingdao*.

51 *DONGHAI* ROAD

Building 11, Suite 1102
a frenzy of sounds
horns, toots, bells, voices
reminded me of a saxophone
floating bebop in my head.

Below were squeaking brakes
a continual din of traffic
    new Hondas, Fords, and a few Mercedes
    old trucks spewing thick black smoke
        as if they were ancient black dragons of mythical mystical powers
    too-heavy carts toppling with fresh fruits, vegetables, and arduous labor
        poverty in optimistic people determined and pushing forward to market
all going home at the end of the day
smiles amid sounds.

Crowded buses lurched to avoid careless drivers and pedestrians
old and new, youth and elders
self-proclaimed independence amid authority.

Suddenly a sequence of precariously close calls
caution thrown to the wind, vehicles hovered beside each other almost intimately.
My fear fled—high whispers of adventure and success beckoned in the craws of the noise.

Toward the tall sky
dragonflies darted like UFOs
glided silently up and around the almost-hidden Pavilion of Ample Blessings
mostly unnoticed by the hordes who remain preoccupied
by issues of uncertain survival or dreams of luxurious leanings.

BADAGUAN NEIGHBORHOOD

An ancient German settlement lies to the east of the city
Tall red-tiled roofs, ample gardens
Narrow whispering tree-lined streets
Villas these days still reserved for military and dignitaries
And old prosperous families ensconced by the rocky shores of *Qingdao*.

Chinese wisteria in *Badaguan*
Cascades wildly over old stone walls.

An old noble home is unpainted and noteworthy
Owners dead or forgotten. Inside the south wing
Sit a neglected creaky iron gate and a covered bodega.
An old plum tree stands defiant in fading beauty
Next to the mildewed abandon of this weathered mansion.
Out back by the large scholars' stones
An overgrown rosebush towers, hiding lingering thorned beauty.

Veils of sandalwood incense hint of spirits and a nostalgic prosperous past.
Listen to the sweet musical sounds: a duo piano-and-lute concert drifting from within.

On the north corner, outside the dilapidated main inner gate
Noisy people pass by with cell phones in cars, buses, trucks.
Group minds rush in modern urgency like busy ants
Oblivious to stately tradition, pollution, and early deaths
Eager for Western styles and boutiques at all costs
Profits and prosperity in *Badaguan*.

Forgotten are the *5 Blessings* in the New China:
long life, wealth, health, love of virtue, and a peaceful, natural death.

SKYGATE: *MOUNT LAO*

Follow the paths of *Laoshan*
past the temple
toward the freedom of the clouds.

Mists and fog are the lovers
of *Laoshan*.
Peaks reach up to the heavens.
So strong their penetration
none can intervene.

Behind hanging curtains of clouds
quiet valleys in negligees of bright wildflowers
snuggle in glens of bamboos and tall pines.

The thin waving veils
of northern clouds are alluring
to the seeker
captured in jade moments
seduced by the shadows
suggesting boundless joys
and pools of possibilities
at the craggy heights.

Before, behind, above, below
the mesmerizing veils dance
creating symphonies of shadows on stone
refreshing the tired traveler.

A mysterious welcome inserts itself.
Illusions of east mountain fairies
hide morning sun-fire and steaming waters.

Above the fog and misty rains
on glowing slants of green light
soar the meditations of the monks.
Rainbows are caught in gusts of wind.
Waterfalls flying like birds and angels
suddenly disappear.

The dawn bell tolls, inspiring my visit.
Its resonance travels with the voices of the
chanting devotees
across the threshold of the trees.

The mountain ridges invite the climber
to sit down with the likenesses of immortal
stone sages
and embrace the stillness.

Mists roll in and out like silver sky curtains
invading the spectacular jade stage.

Pure spring water is abundant
and exploited:
Laoshan Mineral Water, Tsingdao beer
and special harvest green tea
all famous and exported around the nation
and beyond.

Turn toward the golden eastern shore
watch the sunrise and the moonrise
golden light on the welcoming sea.
The soul rises up to sing the joys
of *Laoshan*.

SHROUDED IN SILENCE

High above
at *Laoshan* dwells a world profound
where mountains and waters meet
shrouded in silence
a home of cathedral spirits
and hardworking *gongmin*.

The traveler comes
faces west to refresh the soul
able to laugh, unable to speak.

A solitary cloud can float
for 1,000s of *li*
then disappear without a trace.

Cranes come and play for a season
then fly away
reminding of separation.

Bamboo, wise pines, and glowing magnolias
can be found together
in sparkling veils of rain mists and ruby sunrises.

Rainbows abound
angels in summer's sounds.
Waterfalls dance to unscripted sonatas.
Their eternal final falling
flows freely to the China Sea.

Animals and forms lay hidden
mysterious etudes in green stone.
Red poems in northern-style calligraphy
are waiting to be carved out
in the caring hands of artists.

I dream to return
to *Laoshan* in summer soon
a compendium of hidden communities in Nature's splendor.

APRICOT PICKING

That day, *Laoshan* was a holy place
the district fertile with sparkling water
fruits copious and mountains green as jade.

A rocky ride in 2 old battered cars
over uncompleted new thoroughfares
our boisterous caravan twisted and lurched
past the rocky hazards
and women who sat calmly
on the side of the unpredictable road
selling piles of apricots, large as nectarines.
Our group gathered at the farmer's house
across the bridge and up a narrow lane.

The village was small
the inhabitants and neighbors curious
strolling back and forth past our unfamiliar group.
We were invited to pass through the kitchen
to the back house for sleeping and living.

The farmer's handsome son was cooking.
His father talked with visitors in Chinese
passed around baskets of apricots
served endless refills of *Laoshan* green tea
white-lightning whiskey *jiu* and 12 quarts of *pijiou* beer in between
to be slowly consumed
while 8 of us waited hungry for the long meal to come.
From the chicken pen up the terraced hillside
we feasted on hard-boiled eggs and preserved black eggs
fresh chicken wings and the zesty delicacy of chicken feet.

The pretty, delicate daughter-in-law who served us
had just returned from *Sichuan* that morning
with spicy pork kebab delights.
Next came the preserved meat rolls
the fat bee grubs, fried to perfection
dishes of spinach, tomatoes, fresh ginseng, and cucumbers
all from the garden near the apricot orchard above.
There was *baozi* made with sweet-potato dough
small fried fish, *gala* clams, cornbread, and more.

After the eating and drinking
laden with baskets, we
climbed the hot mountainside
in the metal heat of the summer day
past the 40 or so chickens.
We took pictures then trudged up to the apricot orchard
where 12 large baskets were quickly filled with
orange apricots and brown eggs to take back to the city.

The urban children were afraid to walk past the chickens
and the big, mean-looking dog
so the grownups held their hands and shooed the animals away.
All were delighted to pick vegetables and apricots
and help gather eggs.
After an hour or so, we began to descend
stopping to rest at the cool house which we had passed going up.

Later, we sat on the family *kang*
drinking bottled water from the springs in *Laoshan*.
After that, we arrived back at the narrow lane
where small tables and stools were brought out
to rest again from the heat and have bottomless cups of tea.
We sat under the capacious trees, near the almost-dry riverbed
where the little ones and parents soon went to cool off.

Finally, at the end of the day
bidding fond farewells, we piled into the old cars with baskets brimming
crossed the bridge and retraced our route over the sometimes treacherous roads.
We sang or dozed, hot, dusty, and happy as the summer days are bright and long.

THE NEW *DAXUE*

A phone call from an old friend at the brand-new *daxue*
brought an invitation to share her extraordinary *guanxi*.

While riding the *daxue* shuttlebus, I witnessed
Yet another valley under development.
More roads scratched further swathes of bleeding earth
Cutting through *hutong*, destroying their histories.

Over boulders and loose dirt
Hugging the recently dug-up mountainside
The new road not yet leveled
The cumbersome bus
Almost rolled off the cragged hairpin curve
Into the mountainous jade dust before suddenly coming to
A newly paved strip of road.

We arrived on time for a *guanxi* meeting with faculty
At the new international east campus of *Qingdao* University.
My surprise overflowed at the tennis courts and modern buildings
Olympic swimming pool and meticulously planted pathways.

I met my old friend joyfully
And greeted a former student, too!
They and her staff greeted me warmly.
They bestowed precious access to e-mail
In the state-of-the-art Language and Media Center
And led my tour of the Faculty Lounge and the magnificent campus.

Too soon, we said *zaijian* and took another rocky ride, down the precarious hillside.
This time felt safer in a colleague's shiny black Lexus
Our destination: a familiar restaurant
Near the beach and the famous coastal rock *Shi Lao Ren*.
Dozens of *xiaojie* servers
Attractively dressed in short black skirts, long-sleeved white blouses, and ties
Were ready to serve 100s, though only 30 customers were there on our arrival.

Fuzzy memories of this restaurant
Played like a *qin* on my heartstrings.
I had gone there several years previous
For a surprise farewell party
Hosted by my 15 Chinese students
All mid-level businessmen
On their hazard-filled way to Zambia in Southern Africa
To manage a government-subsidized textile factory.

And now 6 years later
A college administrator, a fellow professor, and I
Were feasting in the same place
On 7 dishes of various fresh seafood delights
And 2 quarts of *Tsingdao* beer.

Savoring this restaurant's spicy tastes once again
I reflected on the generous offer of my friend, now Assistant Dean
Who had just offered me an open-ended job of modest stipend
Teaching English for anywhere from 4 weeks to 1 year at the new *daxue*
Sweetened with free housing, food, and friendship
My *guanxi* presenting an opportunity for the future, due to favorable connections.

LANCUN

I

Countryside found me
riding the back roads at *Lancun*
soon-to-be suburbia
visiting friends' homes then City Hall
sipping tea at each stop
me trying to talk trash in Chinese
needing an interpreter.
We laughed together
visited a new shoe factory
trying on shoes, shoes, shoes
in the village.
Curious workers and their friends
gave me 2 pairs of high heels
made on location in *Lancun*
home of Nike
where I lost my green flowered purse
astrological interpretations
and a bit of myself.

Walking in the market that night
set up in the middle of the street
I bought souvenirs before turning in
listening to men play cards
after midnight in the alleyway
between the rows of houses and walls.
I slept on an old-style *kang* bed.

II

Eating fresh peaches, plums, apricots
crawfish and prawns jumping in the bowl
grubs and other unknown dishes
I enjoyed the cuisine
the fellowship
and the laughter of *Lancun*.

After an early walk to the school
where the young men played soccer
releasing energy in fierce competition
I found a space to chant
the arrival of the day
with the birds
and early breeze
near the rose gardens
under the square of cascading willow trees.

I sat still facing the east
and the bright statue of *Guan Yin*
her arm gracefully raised
hands open to the sky.

I was almost hidden by the purple *lotus* pond
marveling at the colors of peach blossoms
around the Wisteria Pavilion
until you found me ready to go home
happy within.

GOLFING AT JIMO ON SATURDAY

On short notice, we left home early Saturday
In your new Honda to go shopping in *Jimo*.
We stopped and waited twice
for 2 of your friends
before leaving our haven by the China Sea
to head inland and due west.

We followed the road to *Lancun* for a while
then veered off toward *Jimo*
which is known for its marketplace
bustling with people, vendors, cars—
plus all of the shops open at sunrise.

I wanted to explore and compare the merchandise
but since you drove and decided the way
we stopped off instead to meet some officials and city leaders
drank tiring cups of tea, ate fresh peaches and grapes
while sitting at wide tables
in an oversized conference room with large, long windows.

The leaders in this case were all women!
I sat in silence, a foreign *waiguo*
an outsider looking in, listening
to unfamiliar tones of a cacophonous language
a guest lacking understanding
of the swirling words which were dancing
and laughing all around me.

Suddenly, we were up and moving again
by now a small caravan of cars, full of flowers, fruits, and boxes
to visit your dear friend and colleague
recently back home in *Jimo* after brain surgery in *Shanghai*.

We stopped outside the century-old walls of a *hutong*
at a small home—semi-modern, tidy, and comfortable.
I did not visit the bathroom inside
not wanting to stand up old-style and pee.

Again, we were offered ripe peaches and cool drinks by her daughter.
We listened sympathetically as she spoke
in quiet but intense tones
the story of her sudden tumor
its removal and her slow recovery.

Unexpectedly, we were soon off again.
This time, I asked if we were going shopping
but received no answer, and the caravan proceeded
to a Country Club and golf links, to my ultimate surprise.

With excitement and expectation, we got shoes and clubs
lined up and hit the balls on the driving green over the gentle hills
beyond the parking and crowd of elegant cars
surrounded by sophisticated people who laughed loudly and dressed garishly.
For some of us, it was the first time golfing.

In between players, I smoked Chinese cigarettes
Double Happiness, Royals, Hong Mei, Hatamen, all available and freely shared.
After we finished, our caravan continued to a new restaurant
where we ate for 2 hours like royalty.
Even the mayor and vice-mayor dropped by to *ganbei*!

After lunch, we rushed back to *Qingdao*.
Although slightly irritated and late for afternoon appointments
having to reschedule with friends
I did not regret that unpredictable day
when we visited *Jimo*, even though we never shopped at the popular market.

VISITING *HANGZHOU*

The wind sweeps the shores of West Lake
conjures rhythmic sounds of lapping water.

From the oars of the dragon boats
magical *mandala* appear and disappear.

Bamboo leaves rustle at the Shimmering Splendor Pavilion
As thought-shadows create a silken sacred dance.

On the nearby tea plantation
patient workers labor in sizzling summer heat.

Enchanting *Hangzhou* offers surprises in quiet moments.

HANGZHOU LULLABY

Hazy chords of blues and greens, sky and trees
accompany birds' sweet songs of leisurely flight and freedom.

Tall bamboo trees click percussion in the balmy breeze.
Willow leans like a contemplating lover above the cool silver surface.
Solitary blue heron sits on a pole staring at the water.
Crickets chirp, castanets throughout the day—interrupting silent intervals.

Dragon boats glide lazily back and forth, ferrying tourists to the aria of the lake.
A chorus of ducks flies like a breath of intricate choreography
across the stage of distant mountains that tower like gods
peaks screened by the lavender-veiled soft tunes of clouds and mists.

I wander impromptu into the Chinese resort area on the far side of the lake
auxiliary of restricted condos, gated homes, swimmers in bikinis
a secret status playground for government officials and army officers.
Here concerts and parties held for privileged *red princes and princesses* are hidden
invisible to peasants, factory workers, and tourists.

The shaded lanes, freshly painted walls, and gates offer surprise.
Subtle *feng shui* works the magic of correspondences and free harmonies.
A yellow-and-black monarch butterfly dances an adagio close by
like a ghost fearlessly brushing my brown arm.
Jade bamboo leaves fall and float like silent songs on the lake
soon to become a fading concert under a hot yellow cymbal of sunrise.

Inspiration of black-and-white swans on the lake
an ivory moment passes on a wind current, quiet as a sacred song
a wink of presence, silent as a fluttering eye
a flirtatious largo of dance and surprise.

In the distance, blaring noise clashes the mood
traffic, offices, jackhammers, construction cranes, and cars
creating a fractious harmony of progress and memory of water-concerts in Nature.

ALL BECAUSE OF A CIGARETTE!

Finally, I'm sitting down at the airport in *Qingdao*
safe at last. Too much craziness, a *cauchemar*
speeding by, yet in slow motion—my hurried departure!

The day started out slow and easy
sky clearing after the deluge.
My hostess forgot I was leaving.
Somehow, I was not surprised.
Her daughter left early for school. She went to work.
I had tea with her Mama.

My friends, Ming and Tianhua, arrived early, as I had requested
almost 4 hours before departure time, and we set out for the 20-minute ride to the airport.

What happened?
A quick crescendo
too fast—too unbelievable!

When we were almost to the airport
at the toll gate, just after paying
Ming thoughtlessly lit up a *Red Flake* cigarette.
(Later, I would learn that drivers can't smoke on toll roads in China.)
Tianhua and I were in the second row of seats in the small old van.
My voluminous luggage filled mainly with gifts was piled in the back.
A policeman on the side of the road
observed my dark face, an obvious foreigner
and, studying Ming's cigarette, signaled him to pull over.
To my surprise, Ming ignored him, kept smoking, and drove away!

Suddenly, we were being followed
by 4 policemen in an unmarked car
driven by the officer who'd flagged us at the toll gate.
They again signaled Ming to pull over.
Once more, Ming ignored them, and he sped up.
They kept catching up, yelling, indicating for us to stop.

I became thoroughly scared as an incomprehensible chase ensued.
Ming tried to elude them, weaving in and out of highway traffic
blowing his horn for other cars to move and let us over
blocking the neighboring lane so the police could not pass.
The authorities finally got out in front, cutting off the car ahead
forcing it to come to a screeching halt, with us almost crashing into them!

Then 3 of the police leaped out of their car
with menacing looks in official uniforms and purposefully wielding batons.
Instead of getting out to talk to them
Ming suddenly backed up
made a quick u-turn into oncoming traffic
and sped off in the opposite direction away from the airport.
I was having a terror-fit, fearing death at any moment.
Cars scattered all around us as we rushed toward them, dodging.

Tianhua and I were yelling, begging him to stop.
I wanted to get out immediately.
Ming was like a man possessed, hunched over the steering wheel
smoking, speeding, defying the odds and official outcome.

After barely missing several head-on collisions
there was a narrow crossover to the other side
and our minivan swerved across 3 lanes and entered the highway
still heading away from the airport.

Ming hurriedly explained as he drove
we could take a cross-road and connect with another
back to the airport, so he hurried us along
when, surprise, the police were with us again
and the chase continued dangerously, in and out, round about
but at least we were no longer going against the flow of oncoming traffic.
Afraid to look back, I tightly held Tianhua's hands.

With no forewarning, we hurtled again across 3 lanes to an off-ramp.
Down we went, and we lost them.
Suddenly, Ming made a sharp u-turn and headed back into on-coming traffic!
Under the freeway we sped. Again, cars and trucks scattered, until
about a kilometer away, we found another cross-over.

We followed the street
across mud puddles and ponds left from the passing typhoon the day before.
We sped past people riding bikes
some carrying large bundles on their backs or the front or rear of their bikes
and others tugging behind their small bikes large, lumbering peddlers' carts.
All around, fields and low-lying areas were flooded.
The police were nowhere in sight.

Suddenly, the street ended at a 1-lane dirt road used by rural traffic.
It was on a levee, so water was all around. It felt dangerous
as we proceeded onward into the path of an on-coming truck
inching along the narrow way.
2 vehicles could not pass. Ming did not want to reverse
so we both kept moving closer to one another.
There was no question that the truck could not back up.

Ming saw a house to the right
with a new cement pad, all clean. An outdoor kitchen? A family space.
He pulled in the u-access and drove across the man's spotless cement pad
while the man rushed out, angrily, frantically, wildly warning
waving us away and off
finally running and grabbing a lead pipe
then hitting the van.
Wham! Wham! Wham!

He swung with all of his force, as hard as he could.
Lucky for us, he missed the windows
while we sped across his well-tended property
leaving behind muddied tire tracks
as we fled his previously pristine driveway.

For a moment, I thought Ming would get out and fight with the man
for banging his van, but he kept on driving doggedly forward.
We bumped along the deep potholes
mud flying, full of trepidation and slivers of hope.
I was still holding Tianhua's hand.

The levee ended, and there was another paved road
rutted and strewn with runoff from the rains.
Miraculously, Ming saw a taxi and flagged it down.
The young driver was a woman with white gloves
which seemed so ironic in the midst of all the mud and dirt.
He hurriedly conferred with her
told us to get in the cab and threw my baggage in the back
instructing her to get us to the airport as soon as possible
and telling Tianhua he would wait for her there.

We said a hurried good-bye.
I was glad to be in another vehicle
praying not to miss my plane, ready to go home
yet dreading the typical long lines at Customs and fearing
possible repercussions should our adventure be discovered.

On our way to the airport, Ming called Tianhua on her cell
asked her to explain to me that the reason
he did not take me all the way
was that the police would surely be waiting at the airport
since they had ample time to take his license number.

He spoke to me personally and apologized for the ride
said the police were country bumpkins and corrupt.
He said they'd have taken my belongings and passport for a bribe.
Tianhua agreed but explained that his temper often got him in trouble.
I truly contemplated the word "trouble" for the first time in my life.

I doubted his assumptions. How would he know?
What was going on?
Was doubting Chinese police like Blacks fearing white cops in Alabama?

Late, I went through Customs, boarded the plane, and flew out of China
whispering a prayer of gratitude for life and good friends.

In the end, I crossed the China Sea, arriving at Japan's *Narita* Airport.
Qingdao was to the north now, feeling very far away.
Waiting for my flight to *Honolulu*, unexpectedly, I got bumped to first class.
Then, at last, I landed home, met by family, happy and secure on arrival in America.

Wo shi meiguoren.
Hei meiguoren.

III

MAZE HAZE GAZE

A Rush to the Top

STANDING OUT WHILE IN CHINA

My Black skin is conspicuous.

In China, individualism is embargoed, yet influenced by
media, visitors, foreign factories, and studies abroad
curious and clever youths push to expand, experiment, explore.

Sharing the mountains and oceans, everyone seeks acceptable boundaries.

Youths recognize freedom, bypass bans to sites like Facebook
view bootlegged movies and read banned Western books
watch world soccer, and American basketball and football.

Youths distinguish Blacks as creative agents of vanguard influences
imagine possibilities for sepia collaboration and ebony partnerships.

China's stark and promising diversity births allurement in my soul.

I feel like a grain of black sand
a diminutive *carbonado* diamond
a welcomed prize trusting an unknown path of throbbing humanity.

UNDER *BEIJING* SKIES

Somber summer sky frames all of the ancient temples
pavilions in reds, blues, greens—with shades of white
meandering pathways through Chinese conifers and purple bamboo groves.

In gardens, large ornamental rocks
accompany graceful sprays of orchids
designed for observation and reflection.

China's legacy of aesthetics survives in neighborhoods of every modern city.

I sit idly underneath the ample eaves of Dawn Cloud Pavilion
beyond memory and imagination
discovering essences of interconnections
staring out at a lily pond
substantial leaves cushioning magnificent magenta *lotus* flowers.

People wake up slowly under *Beijing* skies
noise-pace-bustle
breath-quickening
crescendos all around me
toward the advancing day.

Humid, heavy, hanging haze
dusty, drab, damp, dreary thoughts
misty, muggy, mysterious emotions
coarse diesel fumes hang in the summer air.

Nearby, umbrellas dance and jostle
across the graceful arch of Marble Moon Bridge
people busily going to market before work
to buy fresh sustenance for their noonday meals.

Footsteps muffle on stone with the growing noise
whistles, voices, trucks, horns, sirens, trains—amid gridlock.

Remnant sounds in diminishing clarity first clash then melt
into cacophonous music of postmodern humanity under *Beijing* skies.

DOUBLE GLORY PAVILION AND THE COMMUNIST PARTY

Dawn finds me meditating at the classically constructed Double Glory Pavilion.

I hear
a bicycle swish by on wet pavement, the rider singing a quiet song.
I hear
10,000 splashing froglets, each smaller than a fingernail on wet leaves.
I hear
wind rustling in the willow groves, fragile freshness in the quiet the morning.

Abruptly, at that precise moment, the Party voice preempts tranquility.

On every corner, the daily announcement blares from public radios
remind me of my country's Civil Defense sirens warning of hurricanes
but in China the deafeningly loud news broadcasts awaken city dwellers.

The leaders dare the public to ignore the governmental transmissions
conquer silence, defeat personal thought, and deconstruct intimate meditative moments.

MORNING PUBLIC ANNOUNCEMENT

At exactly 6 every morning
The announcer's voice and music intrude
Into every corner of the sprawling city
Stalking the pre-dawn darkness
Officials smug in their power to disrupt the personal.

Circumventing peace, the broadcast rips the daybreak air.

Most citizens are up and about.

Groups of elders clap to rouse their circulation
Quickly walk forward and backward, then stroll tranquilly.

A few chat quietly or noisily before and after the voice
But most remain silent during the daily event
Moving individually like shadow dancers
Before joining the tangled multitudes.

The voice of the public announcement
Overpowers noise from blaring car and truck horns
Overwhelms tooting taxis trying to get fares
Overshadows pedestrian conversations
From children's chatter to angry adult discourse.

Millions on the go, moving earth, building skyscrapers
Creating new roads, cars, machines, businesses
But with lingering attitudes of submission to authority
Pause, stop activities, and reverently listen to the official public information.

The coded message: be invisible, let the leaders rule, restore the virtues.

Everywhere the eye roams
Knotted new buildings and roads rest
Unfinished, uninhabited
Falling into disrepair
Unreliable water, phones, communication, and email.
At my work, the classrooms are dark and dank
And the plumbing ancient, with scores of leaky pipes.

Day after day, the hazy skies fill with fog
Dust from the distant *Gobi* desert
And smog from *Beijing*'s countless cars.

In my apartment, the TV features
Sports from soccer to basketball, tennis to ping pong
Dance pageants
Lousy American movies with old stereotypes of Blacks
Modern Chinese soaps
Traditional tales of ghosts and dragons
Concerts with *qin* zithers and *pipa* lutes
And endless segments praising government activities:
Ceremonies for more new buildings
Highways, dams, children's projects
Military and educational activities
Always accompanied by red flags, banners, kerchiefs, and armbands.
The building supervisor from the *Neighborhood Party Committee*

A community-based government functionary
Listens, observes, and reports errant behavior.

The voice, collective for billions, invades each morning
Promoting the power of the Party and the supremacy of the nation
Reaching every corner, creak, crevice.
Announces itself during cooking, eating, tea drinking, lovemaking
Stomps into gloomy shadows and gray Soviet-style buildings
Marches into preparations for work and school, forgetting no one.

The propaganda voice ensnares, deludes
Under weary clouds
Controlling, playing with minds
Children, grandfathers, grandmothers
Parents, friends, coworkers
Hierarchies of officials
Molded by a subtext of Confucian tradition and totalitarian rule.

Before early-morning marketing, *taiji*, or calisthenics
Everyone listens (or pretends to pay attention to)
The voice, the news, and the National Anthem: "The East Is Red."

I marvel at survival: incredible porcelain, silk, jewelry, architecture.
Reverently respected, family structures endure.
Poor and rich, from young to elderly, submit to authority
Yet circumvent prescribed, adulterated virtues and values.

People stare endlessly at my dark skin and colorful garments.

In the cities, Nature struggles
Too few gardens, too little clean water, not enough *bodhi* trees.
In the markets, cymbidiums are cheap, gardenias prohibitive.

The beautiful parks suffer stunted growth, too much pollution.
Smiles warm the heart.
Food delights the senses.
Peonies and kindness inspire love.

China is great.
China is growing.
China is a maze.
China is a paradox.
China is a puzzle.
China is indecipherable.
China is deep in my blood.

STRENGTH IN A GRAY CITY

Purple clouds and lavender mists shroud
Leagues of drab and dreary apartment buildings.

Glass porches protect clothes drying on urban laundry lines.
Plants peek out from plain pots: roses, *bonsai*, loquats.

Monochrome hordes mask colorful individuals
As all surge through hazy, dust-crowded streets.

Ancient history rides the echoing winds
While perennial sands whistle down from the *Gobi* desert.

Coal powders everything from homes to factories
As people choke/cough/spit/swallow/repeat.

They work hard. They smoke *Yun Yan* and *Red Flake*.
They talk on cell phones, ride bicycles, wait for buses.

Exceptional ones care about healing the environment.
Others care only for money, selling survival at all costs.

The people are strong and purposeful; dialectical forces persevere.

$ELLING $URVIVAL

An ancient land grown modern
juxtapositions of organized wisdom
trucks, cars, taxis, *pedicabs*, bicycles
carts pulling wares piled high
throngs traversing noisy streets
vendors selling survival for *yuan*
gadgets, fake designer goods, pirated CDs
gritty gray air, crowded city spaces
heavy loads carried into the future—
pollution belies transformation, more than a billion strong.

HOT LIKE A *WOK*!

Blazing sun passes through intricate mazes of city streets.

Then thick clusters of dark clouds reveal patches of pale blue sky.

Myriad skyscrapers stand like ghosts, etched across the languid horizon.

Surreal performance of frenetic progress pauses as Nature gathers force.

Thunder cracks suddenly, exploding in my ears. *Beijing* is hot like a *wok*!

TOWERING *BEIJING* CRANES

1,000 cranes in *Beijing* today
Perched precariously
Turning slowly
Deliberately lifting and placing
Heavy loads
24 hours a day
7 days a week
On 1,000 buildings
Most more than 30-stories tall
While builders, welders, carpenters, plumbers, electricians
Work at maximum speed and capacity
On the turbulent great dash
To complete bodacious big projects before the 2008 Olympic Games.

ARCHITECTURE EXTRAVAGANZA

Beijing buildings amaze
Joined by corridors and passages, stairs and walkways.
Geometrical glass windows and doors
Display astonishing patterns in blues, greens, and golds.

Tops of buildings exhibit irregular lighted protrusions
Penthouses, towers, antennas, pyramids, pagodas.

Buildings have original trim like insets and carved, flying eaves.
Buildings have semi-circles with curved sides and wavy roofs.
Buildings have irregularly angled fronts, backs, sides, windows, entries.
Brick buildings come in mauve, white, black, gray, pink, peach
Dark red, walnut brown, taupe, green, aquamarine, and tangerine!

A few select buildings feature
Marble or porcelain tiles
Unique round towers, bay windows
Enormous, extravagant, sparkling chandeliers
90-degree triangles facing each other
Rectangular forms with rounded sections
And 50-story skyscrapers flaunt glass walls up and down 3 sides.

Buildings astound foreigners and *gongmin* alike
But what happens with earthquakes or *typhoon*s when safety codes are ignored?

MASTERS OF ALLUREMENT

With magical lights, the Chinese are masters of allurement:

Small and large publicity signs adorning every metropolis
Lights 40-stories up at the crowns of ever-taller buildings
Rectangles and disks, the gaudy and the subdued
Across the middles of buildings and down low on the sides

Backgrounds flaunting flowing lights
Depicting bodies of water, sunrises, beaches
Geometrical shapes in cubes, triangles, spheres
Foregrounds parading business names and messages
Displayed in Chinese calligraphy or Romanized *pinyin*
Lights flashing, running, twinkling, circling
10,000 tiny white bulbs on cylinders 8-stories tall

Lights artistically arranged on bars, nightclubs, discos
Showing palm trees, bottles, pineapples, music notes, and the sun
Strings of lights on alternate balconies of luxury buildings
Beneath every other window, lights in immense highrises
In celeste, chartreuse, harlequin, lavender, rose, and bright red

Lights on the rails and sides of freeways and overpasses
Lights accentuating the flowers that line streets and highways
Lights in red lanterns outside small 6-table restaurants
Lights fronting stores and hotels, strings stacked in climbing rows
Lights along escalators, tiny lights in elevator floors and on the walls
Lights 1-story high wrapping a restaurant that feeds 1,000 people
Lights at *Tiananmen Square*, the *Emperor's Palace* and the *Forbidden City*.

Chinese city lights make American Christmas lights seem insignificant!

But around 10 p.m. across China, 12 million apartments go mostly dark
As the world's most practical people turn in, sleeping early
Preparing for survival, the inevitable competition, and the next advancing day.

MODERNIZATION PROJECTS

Construction everywhere, train tracks, roads, bridges, buildings
Hard work to neutralize garbage, pollution, and poison
China rushes to modernize and outshine the U.S. and Europe.

Towering electric poles march through Northeast China
Support straight power lines that glimmer in the sun
Connect necessary voltage for shining towns and cities
Sending light to terminals of technology for more than 100s of millions.

Tall, bright streetlights line large highways
Jam-packed with imported luxury cars
Snarled in traffic on the ring roads around yet another new city.

Multiple colonies of erected cranes displace communities and destroy *hutong*
Awkward juxtapositions, fragile emotions along waterways of weeping willows.

At least 10,000 new buildings spinning out of control
5-stories tall and 7-10 units on each floor
House new industrial workers.

And 20-story natural gas towers, wide as 2 tractor-trailer trucks
Supply voracious large cities with fuel to cook traditional Chinese dishes.
Coal furnaces belch bogs of billowing white smoke, heat and energy for the masses.

THE ART OF SURVIVAL

Tear down the old! Build the new!
Pay off officials, watchdogs, planners, permit givers!

Architects' dreams come true—especially buildings at least 20 stories.
The New China near *Wei Feng* features exotic shapes and artistic styles.

Glass windows outweigh their cement structures
Gorgeous blues, forest greens, brassy golds.
Buildings stand tall and statuesque like obelisks
Or short and round like mushrooms
House the countless new banks, hotels, offices, business headquarters
        Insurance firms, real-estate companies, condos for the wealthy.

Red calligraphy artfully adorns the buildings' tops and sides.
Plentiful rooftop lights announce their enormous and spectacular presence.

POWER AND PRESTIGE

Concrete and brick buildings
Cement highways and bridges
Everywhere present
Built to endure, yet . . .
Torn up, broken down, rebuilt
Another week, another season
Another building, another need
Bigger, stronger, better.

On the road to *Laoshan*
2-story villas hastily constructed for new billionaires
Replace the humble *hutong* of generations of fishermen
Mimicked elegance provides vacation homes
Where wealthy businessmen, high government and military officials
Come for a few days or weeks a year.
Otherwise, the dwellings lay empty, not rented out.

Where do displaced families live after power and prestige move in?

INDUSTRIAL ZONES

About 3 hours from *Qingdao*, a rainstorm follows speeding trains.

The 100s of heavily laden coal cars move to and from industrial zones.

Teams of workers load and unload materials
for menacing plentitudes of oil refineries, natural gas tanks, and gigantic coal towers.

Smokestacks are everywhere
tall, thin, and straggly like toothpicks or rockets
marked with red-and-white circles
flooding the sky with smoke
blanketing the city with toxins
dotting the skyline like dangerous ghosts.

Pollution seeds the air with poisonous acid rain, and the water is unsafe.
Who dares to eat the fruits and vegetables grown near this populated place?
Yet humanity overcomes the most awful conditions, survives and thrives, for a while.

RED FLAGS

After *Jinan*, before *Tianjin*, and toward *Beijing*
miles and miles of flatland agriculture
has been put into intensive production.

The 1,000s of *hectares* of low greenhouses
sit covered with white translucent plastic
and topped with illimitable red flags.
Unimaginable amounts of fruits and vegetables
fed with sprinklers and pesticides provide sustenance for millions.

Camouflaged gardens stretch as far as the eye can see
on both sides of the speeding train
interrupted only by small clusters of trees
and a few houses with red-tiled roofs.

Fertilizer factories abound
all in the name of the efficient production of the food supply.

Where does the irrigation water come from?
Where are the bees sipping crimson peonies?

The *5 Celebrated Fruits*
plums, apricot, peaches, chestnuts, dates
grow high on the hillsides.

The *4 Gentlemen of Flowers*
plum blossoms, chrysanthemums, bamboo, cymbidium
are far away.

The *5 Blessings*
long life, wealth, health, virtue, and a peaceful natural death
lie buried in pollution and the powerful push to get wealthy.

Technology and chemical factories trump temples, gardens, and pagodas.
Loyalty, excellence, and cultivation of refinement and the arts are devalued
abandoned like *hutong*, forgotten like virtues, unobserved like precious rituals.

Priceless pilgrimages, disciplined courtesies, and *guanxi* are lost to progress.

CHINA'S FOOD SUPPLY

In Eastern China
Cities, towns, factories, industry
National fields of agriculture
Small plots of uncultivated land here and there
No private farms or farm animals to be seen
Big people power to feed and be fed—
1/4 of the earth's population
Resides in this enormous economic zone.

Nearby, on the edge of a collective *hectare*
Spotless yellow backhoes, tractors, and trucks collect dust.
With gasoline unaffordable, few get to use them.
They look almost ridiculous in their bright yellow idleness
Next to farmers working diligently nearby
With hoes, sickles, and buckets of hand-carried water.

Mounds of golden wheat stand tall
Waiting to be cut and threshed on remote paved roads
In the season of sun and harvest.
Farmers bend low to weed, cultivate, and cut
Lean forward to hoe, kneel to plant and transplant
Use their strong backs, legs, arms, and their rough hands to grow food.

Sometimes, one can see a couple together in tandem with a plow.
The man wears a chest harness, pulling like horse, mule, or ox.
The woman guides from behind the narrow plow in straight rows.
Both are happy to prepare the soil and watch the crops mature.

After work and school, all the citizens, from children to seniors
Toil in the government-appointed collective fields
And then work their small private gardens before the hard-earned evening meal.

EXECUTIVE OFFICE

Across from the broad, busy walkway
punctuated with stylized, bigger-than-life stone statues
past the music park veiled by summer fog
which boasts the world's largest piano
near the beach preparations in full swing
to host the 2008 Olympics
just beyond *Wu Si Square*
with a towering red sculpture and spectacular fireworks
high above the children's park
near the lavish celebration of the Ocean Festival . . .

I sit in a friend's spacious executive office in the new City Hall
amid black leather elegance, air-conditioning shielding me from summer heat.

The bright room hosts a classic blue-silk carpet
2 ample couches
6 comfortable armchairs
a massive mahogany desk
nanmu cedar cabinets
and artfully placed tables.

A *fuwuyuan* tea server supplies important officials, foreign businessmen, and guests
the spring-harvest green tea prepared with fresh, heated-to-perfection *Laoshan* water.

On the northern wall hangs a strikingly large still-life painting of
an antique porcelain vase holding a bright bouquet of yellow-and-blue flowers.
In the eastern corner, a potted plant as wide as the wingspan of an eagle
renders a light fresh feeling, and the office provides an ample view of the sea.

A red flag with 5 golden stars
commands attention on the eastern corner of the executive director's desk
which stands in the center of this impersonal space.
Captured paradoxes: crimson patience, golden perseverance
artwork and silver and crystal gifts for special guests
witness the aim of the Politburo to nurture business relations, cultural longevity, and pride.

Politics and economics, comrades and competitors
conspire with conservative values and extravagance
to welcome waiguo, eager investors, CEOs, and ministry and security officials.
On the western wall by the cedar double-door entry
a miniature pine tree bends gracefully, supported by wires
flexible, reliably strong, a marvel of simplicity in time and attention.

Mysterious power resides in the *feng shui* of this executive office.

JINGCHA: THE POLICEMAN

Late afternoon, predictable as a clock, rows of traffic stack up.
a rare traffic policeman stands in the middle of an intersection
on a pedestal, watching, directing, blowing his whistle as needed.

Under his gaze, drivers behave politely
allow other cars to turn bravely across their paths.
Nearly 20 cars pass quickly until he officially halts the transit.
Someone way back leans on a horn, joined by more long blasts.
At last, he permits the automobiles to proceed forward once more.

Presiding above the throbbing rush-hour throngs, the officer
periodically lifts his baton to allow pedestrians to pass.
The river of cars/buses/trucks abruptly stops
And 100s of pedestrians wedge across to catch buses or walk home.
These days, few bicycles are seen in this fashionable part of town.

Over and up the hill, no police, an old section of the city teems
with people on foot, on bikes, and pushing heavy carts
who buy and sell fresh vegetables, fish, meat, fruit, and especially melons.

That was before the frantic pre-Olympic renewal projects and upgrades
when citizens could peacefully visit markets and return home for dinner.

BEWARE THE FLASH

Rain quickly filled the carp and *lotus* pond.
Water suddenly overflowed onto sloped footpaths.
Inspiration flashed like a raging river
gushed like the blast of rain on the night of my 7th day on the coast.

Water wraiths moved around mudslides
and expanding rivers overflowed
that peculiar spring of early monsoons
with the invisible new moon, governess of floods.

Water rushed towards dry streambeds
shivered with flies. Imagining snakes, boas, dragons
I thought it would rage once again in flash flooding.
Without warning, the deluge stopped as quick as a rabbit.

I was left with soaked clothes, ruined shoes
a lunar halo and fertile wet rhymes
barely recognizable tunes, vague omens
visible apparitions below the stormy surface.

No opal moon goddess, no star animals in the mythical heavens
revealed the unwritten unspeakable damage
but small breaks in tall ghost clouds
hovered on the jagged edge of a *typhoon* pushing across the China Sea.

In the not-too-far imagination
verses and water danced and spilled into crooked poems and blurry traditions.
Floods collapsed poorly constructed dams, created unexpected myriad deaths
and demanded conventional sometimes heroic rescues.

The next morning, *bing-le* (sick)! Foreign chills, many sneezes, a high fever.
Friends brought soups, traditional herbal medicine, and special healing teas.
I was saved in 24 hours and ready to go again into my timeless explorations.
Beware the flash!

WHERE WERE YOU LAST NIGHT?

Where were you last night
when the moon was almost full
a gold lantern in the tall summer sky?

Where were you
when the aureate night shimmered
like a dreamtime on the intimate ocean of self?

I missed you when I stood alone at the window.
Smells and touches lingered, gathering sustenance
the begonia memory of our fine day and evening.

We had walked together
shadows in the moonlight, shifting shapes like dancers
stepping lightly, feeling complete
in an uncertain performance of diplomacy and order.

I had been happy as a bird soaring toward the illusive sky
treasuring each moment we shared.
I had imagined balance and harmony
before the wind under my *phoenix* wings disappeared.

Where were you last night?
Suddenly, dangerous times
10 p.m. curfews imposed by the government
180 murders in 3 months
such violence unheard of
in the sleepy sanatorium city and vacation retreat.

Where were you, just before the imminent visit
of the powerful American president?
Who was killing whom, the protesters or the police?
Or maybe it was gangs of thugs and illegal drugs?

Negative opinions cloaked in secrecy, newspapers silent
the rumor mill and monitors kept fear alive
maintaining control, putting a heavy leash on freedom.

The next few days, there was even an occasional loud thumping
a black stealth helicopter, never seen before, an enormous police presence.

Warning! Gossip on the tea vines:
escaped prison gang from the northeast promising to kill 1 person a day
      unless their leader is released from prison
or a renegade seeking to make officials and government look bad
      unable to control dissidents
or another theory, frustrated unemployed workers on a rampage committed the slaughter.

It is a fact that a foreign woman was among those attacked
stabbed in broad daylight on the main street in the sleepy city
(speculation: smuggling national treasures, or a love triangle)
such international violence unheard of for decades.

Hooray for heroes!
Old men playing Chinese checkers near the scene
saw the violence, and feeling a moral duty
picked up their portable folding stools as weapons
and beat the assailant until his left eye fell out.

The woman was detained in the hospital
several weeks after healing
the government aiming to avoid bad publicity
on the eve of Bill Clinton's visit
tensions running tight as a high wire.

So where were you last night?
Not walking with me, not sitting or lounging close by
but in another place
perhaps near the Temple of the Eastern Peak
perhaps looking out from your hotel window
perhaps sleeping, dreaming
remembering precious time shared
foundations laid, links established.

There is no certainty
especially in the time of the full moon
changing tides, planting and growth
floods and factory fires, earthquakes and chemical spills
when summer passes into soft and intimate autumn.

Where were you late last night in a time of danger before my imminent departure?

SATURN WITH A RED SCARF

After work, the sun's departure is magical.
Like Saturn with a scarf, day melts to night.
Colors coalesce: yellows, oranges, and crimson
a poetic final burst of fiery beauty.

From the roof of my 10-story walk-up
I observe the world below
red flags
the ancient and modern
ridiculously juxtaposed
carts and cars, bikes and buses
donkeys and taxis
traditions and innovations
homespun and factory-made
brushes/ink/pens/scribes and home computers.

At dusk, the noise of the city dims with daylight and dinner.
Sunset's arrival and Saturn's scarves melt stark differences
erasing the angular contrasts, softening the angry discrepancies.

At starlight, millions retreat across China
from certain frenzy and jarring paradoxes
into their dwellings and families
to act and feel in the familiar traditional way.

Evening aromas fill the hungry air
as they hurry home to share meals, woes, adventures
eager to taste the ancient recipes and savor each other
before the dawn of new contradictions
and the disciplined rule of Saturn enforced by the red scarf.

IV

VEILED TIME

Visions, Spirits, Loss

ANOTHER LANGUAGE

Peach blossoms speak in fragrance
the trees' wood a charm against evil
in the fertile land of the Middle Country, *Zhongguo*.

They share freely like their sister and brother apricots and almonds
their mysterious ghostly beauty and the gift of longevity
bringing stunning whirls of delicate colors and inspirational meaning
to the pages of the perennial poets: *Du Mu, Du Fu, Li Bai*.

Everyone longs to travel to the jade mountain
to seek the calming hums of tall pines and sycamores
to wait for the solitary song of the mythical *phoenix*
to enjoy the lofty cool whisper of elevated meditation
out of ordinary time, a vibrant language, Nature, and a vital people, *Zhongguoren*.

DRAGONFLIES

A dragonfly circles
pauses in an orange, translucent motion
reminds me of a placid lake in *Hangzhou*

a concert at the tea plantation
a tour at the art school
a shared massage by the mineral pool

where we idled
one summer afternoon when
you swam, ordered expensive drinks, dozed.

Memory circles like an apparition—fades in and out
illusive here and there, transmuted.
I remember
mineral mists, honeybees, and dragonflies
iridescent golden pollen shimmering
with you by my side at the sea.

At that time, we sat on the beach of becoming
hot as a skillet in *Badaguan*.
Magenta neon dragonflies drifted ever higher
to find moisture on a reluctant breeze.

I sought a cool spot to compose a poem
in the shade of a gnarled pine tree
which resembled a dragon of sinuous contortion.

You watched me.
Nearby *lotus* blossoms painted the pond
beside the Flowering Tree Pavilion and Zig Zag Path Concession Stand.

Daring dragonflies with diaphanous wings
flew by like strokes of calligraphy
on a heavy summer canvas, a dazzling display of unruffled, translucent grace.

MYSTICAL *PAGODA*

Through the barred windows of the noisy computer room
across the busy road, beyond the blaring horns
squeaking gears, students' laughter, and ringing bicycle bells
the top of the *5 Blessings Pagoda* catches my eye
symmetrical and serene, shrouded in ghostly mist.

Relative silence floats at the rarely frequented *pagoda*
tucked away in an abandoned rock garden.
Peach tree leaves shadow dance nearby
on the fractured cement ground.

Unfamiliar wrens
joyfully flit, dart, and hide.
Honeybees taste purple nectar
stir up morning-glory delight.

Orange-and-white butterflies float
imagined thoughts on pristine water.
A golden orb mirrors solar-dreams
as a new mood shimmers through the morning fog.

Curious large blue jays and a lone stork
share the overgrown rock garden and forlorn gazebo.

Ragged hedges of mock orange
drop imagined fragrance along untended pathways.
A 30-foot stone sculpture sits in irregularity.
The pond is overgrown with weeds and neglect.

A couple arrives and sits on the cracked benches.
Surprise sun illuminates a corner of morning *lotus* flowers.

I watch a lone cassia leaf
yellow and brown, drifting down an unpredictable path
blowing haplessly in the morning breeze, knowing beauteous freedom.

SEASONAL RESONANCE

An indigo breeze touches my face.
Rest and flight, my tender lover is lost like summer's eaten fruits.

The songs of the seasons ever enchant my ear.
Echoes of voice-rhythms throb in my magenta heart.

Spring. The east wind brings the morning fog.
Summer. Midnight clears the hot south wind.
Fall. The west wind conveys the evening smog.
Winter. The north wind carries the ghosts of snow.

Visions at the Crystal Pool Pavilion
Are perilous to veiled souls.
Dare we show ourselves?

A pampered garden at the *Phoenix* Terrace
Pale imitation of heaven's splendor—why bother with dirt and disorder?

The mantle of misty evening
Reminds me of apparitions, astrology, horoscopes, and numbers
Illusive superstitions of our unknown seasonal destinies.

I thread through traditional paths passing artfully placed ponds
Cleverly hidden from industrial zones and modernization
Contemplating the vagaries of seasons and hearts
Dispassionate pondering in a classical Chinese city, haunted by *feng shui*.

A DAY

Cool morning fog invites the early riser
to visit the spirit of plum blossoms
at the Precious Moon Pavilion
before shadow dancing.

In the afternoons, birds sing
thrill the listener with tiny songs, cheery chirps, caws, and squawks.
They rustle the *gingko* trees
move the tea bushes and camellia air
happy currents in the sun.

Alone with the chill of the evening
waiting for the stars to shine
the night breeze announces itself
caresses the sweet magnolias
releases perfume to the nose of heaven.

Fragrant dreams beckon
in the embrace of the full moon.
Stars struggle to shine in the hazy China night.
The poet contemplates a wilted black rose, practices *mudra*, imitating *Guan Yin*.

NOT ENOUGH TIME

2 days before my departure
I cut short my shopping trip
rushed back to my lodge on the 8th-floor walk-up
only to find an empty space
and disappointment.
You were late.

Another friend came.
You finally arrived.
There were many flocks of feelings.
We had little time together
to talk, to visit.
Swallowing my pain, I pretended
to be happy, light, joyful, generative
missing you in my imagination—the great thief
and then you were gone.

I took a walk to the *Phoenix* Pavilion
trying to catch/interpret/plant each word
mindful that my time was running out, flying away.
I was letting go
you oblivious or stoic.
I passed the hours.
The moon was almost full
and hopefully bright that eventide.

I returned home and finished packing
sat on the roof of stillness
and watched the city lights
alone again
like when I first arrived
contemplating the vagaries of my emotions
the changing moods of impending departure
excitement, anxiety, and even grief
listening to the mysterious music of the wind and stars.

And then morning surprised me.
I was gone quickly, absolutely too soon.

LONGTAN LAKE PARK

At last a park, where I can rest under a tree, on a patch of grass
across from a manmade waterfall and a tall stone sculpture of *Mencius*!
An orange-and-white cat limps by a tiny Buddhist shrine on the hillock.

Photographers scout and scurry with camera crews trailing them
taking wedding pictures all around the scenic park
the soon-to-be married couples elaborately dressed and coiffed.

The lovers are impatient for impending propitious wedding dates
numerically chosen by years, months, and days
selected intentionally by family diviners and fortune tellers, now called social advisors.

Parents, children, and grandparents
seek afternoon entertainment, fish for live gold mollies in a rubber-lined pond
as elders play and laugh, gather paper and paints at small tables to do watercolors.

Duck boats not dragon boats move lazily back and forth
meander among the cascading willows, over the curving shore of lake water
while over there, noisy toy speedboats race in dizzying circles by remote control.

It is hard to find a quiet dry space in the shade.
The grass is wet from watering.
I find a tree and recline, going against the propriety of cultural patterns.

Gazing up at the green parasol of leaves from 7 cypress trees
I suddenly notice 3 fake life-sized coconut trees placed by the waterfall
with garishly painted red, yellow, and green fronds, misplaced in a remote *Beijing* park.

ORACLE BONES AND THE 1998 *TAIWAN* EARTHQUAKE

I

New moon energy
Mercury retrograde
magnetic trouble
earthquake. Great loss!

The first day of autumn
so quiet and still
it caused people to notice and pause.

Evening passed:
people completed their day
and nestled in their beds.

The violent rumbling began
without warning
while you and he slept peacefully
on the 4th floor of the apartment block compound.

Without warning
came the calamitous collapse of the 14-story building
next door. Dust and screams for help
filled the night
the horror unknown
hidden in the absolute darkness.

You, dear friend, scrambled to hide
from the shaking
trying to reach a doorway, or the bathroom
sought to crawl or drag yourself to safety
as cement blocks and tiles flew off the walls
you desperately holding onto the hand of your true love.

Quaking, suffocating, shouting
deafening noise and then
for a few minutes, the earth was eerily still and silent.

II

Your lover remembered the harnesses and pulley
tucked under the kitchen sink for earthquakes
retrieved them in-between the violence
despite his terror at the unpredictable shaking.

Somehow, he assembled the contraption
with a miraculously found flashlight
but you, dear friend, were terrified of heights.

Just the summer before, in *Qingdao*
we had met and bonded
living in an apartment building
assigned to foreigners at the university.
Overcoming your fear of heights, you had daily climbed the stairs
up to my 10th-story lodge and onto the roof where my clothes hung.
We would do *taiji*
in the crimson glow of sunrises or sunsets
or sit together for hours
talking and looking out over the growing city.

III

Another violent shock hit *Jiji* township.
Your love realized you must both escape
but the doors were jammed, and there was no balcony.

You shouted, "Try going 1 floor down!"
Using the harness and pulley
he descended to the 3rd floor
while you, my treasure, watched helplessly
hoping for an escape.

The home below empty, he broke the windows
cut his hands, felt his way through the shattered dark
yet that door out was also jammed.
No easy exit, no escape
except by the dreaded harness and pulley.

IV

He tried to return to you on the 4th floor
wanted to come back in the window.
You would not pull him up
told him to look for another way
perhaps the stairs . . .

You did not say that you were terrified
the height, the night, the dust, the awful screams
so he attempted the harness and pulley once more.

While he hung suspended between floors
another quake shook everything
more damage, screams, falling.
The stop on the pulley gave away.
He fell and fell and then stopped
let go, balled up, dropped to the ground.
You cried.

V

With injured ankles and legs, but alive
he called up to you, climbed over the wall
made his way past rubble to the front of the building
where you waited high at the other window.

Your rational mind took control.
You had to get out, overcome
the fear of heights, of the pulley
of another tremor that could bring down your building
killing you all.

Painfully injured
he tried to find the stairs up
the building so familiar
but they had collapsed
taking with them his last hope.

VI

He called up to you again
weaker now, reluctant to tell you
but you rallied in courage
shouting that you would use the pulley to come down.

He slowly picked his way through the rubble
to the back of the building
and again you waited, ready to descend
both of you convinced the building would soon collapse.

He paused for you to get into the 2nd harness
warning you about free-fall due to the broken pulley
squinting anxiously up into the darkness.

VII

How was anyone to know
that as you began your descent
another violent shaking would begin?
Unable to hold on
you fell, dear friend, down, down, down
hitting your head against a cement wall
and tumbling unconscious to the ground.

After the shaking halted, he found you in the dark
lifted your head, cradling it in his arm.
Underneath, his hand found your fatality
head split open, instant death.

Despite his injuries, he moved you to a flat place
lay down beside you, ready to die with you in the next tremor.
It did not come.

VIII

8 hours later
the rescue squad finally arrived
finding you in his arms.
He was critically injured, deep in shock.

The devastated small city of *Jiji* notified families.

After 3 days, your brother arrived from England
bearing a freezer in which to carry you home.
With 2,500 dead in the city, no coffins were available.

Your lover tried to reach me by email.
You had spoken to him of me
shared my letter, your wish to come to *Hawai`i*
but his email never arrived . . .

Months later, he found me
on a picket line at the University of *Hawai`i*
disclosed the gruesome details of your death.

IX

Dearest Lynn,

I treasure the memories of our shared adventures
intimate conversations, jazz, and books
walks we took along beaches
coffee breaks
shopping excursions
our mutual love of fabrics
visits to the tailor
wearing matching skirts and black silk dresses.

You have gone forever
leaving pictures, clothes, and memories—my friend lost too soon.

DELETERIOUS TIME

The hierarchy of deaf angels
Leaves us with terror of living and dying.

Our temporary home on earth
Exposes habits and expectations
Moments of light laughter.

Springtime flies away so quickly
A piano concert
A soaring song
A flowering almond tree
A lover's embrace
A tranquil sea.

Foggy days, smoggy air, and starless nights
Delete the ancestral vision and virtues
Cast downward to the rubble of new cities.

And then
We wake up terrified
Our fate of emptiness exposed.
Abandoned by parents
Love, logic, guidance
Deleterious time gnaws at our bodies
Stealing youth, beauty, brains.

A desolate unknown
Stretches like a coffin
In a lugubrious procession of venerated rituals.

Dark sobbing at the Pavilion of Broken Dreams
We endure loss and calamity.

Stars conquer the black night.
Poets contemplate hope in veiled time
Writing of wilted rose petals and terror in a chimerical world.

CLOSE QUARTERS

We squabbled.
You came home too late from the land of officials

Sometimes, I empathized with your daughter's needs
your lack of demonstrated love, time, and attention
her silent pain at your inattention.
When I asked, she told me:
"It does not matter. It is my pleasure."

This time you came home from the bureau
did not look at me
but invited me out to a late supper.
Feeling slighted and used
I rejected your invitation with an excuse.

The following evening
I invited you to share dinner with me
my style—eating at home.
Your mother had taught me some Chinese cooking.
I offered eggplant with beef, peanut chicken, poached fish.
You declined, "I don't eat meat"
which we both knew was not true
"but maybe a good salad."
I walked away for a while.

The evening after that, I spent 2 hours preparing a meal
even making a special lychee dessert.
I ate with your daughter. You did not show up.

The next morning, you said you had been with "important people"
government dignitaries and business leaders flown in from afar.

Angry and frustrated
I went out alone to the public square activities.
When you finally came back late that night
I was still gone.

Mixed messages and missed meals, disruptions and hurt feelings in close quarters.

YEARNING FOR SALLY'S GIFTS
(Elegy for Sally, Fang Xue Rong)

Dear Sally,

For nearly 20 years of surprisingly clear and fun friendship, we made vivid pictorial memories.
In person we shared a multitude of adventures.
Separately, we witnessed Hong Kong join China and later the arrival of the millennium.
I remember our discussions about gender and power in *Shandong* Province.
Your spirit is near.

Part I

A strong north winter wind rends the ghostly air
in *Hawai`i*, blowing pain at hearing of your passing.
My beloved Sally
your *dharma* ended too soon.

You left us just before the Year of the Horse 2014 thundered in
boldly, fiercely, loyally toward the Bohai Sea and coast of *Shandong*.

Sister Sally,

Your untimely transition transpired in gentle *Qingdao*
where we had first met, the green island
with misty gardens, superstitions, and a famous sanatorium.
I had been on a mesmerizing tour
with *East-West Center* educators in the *Asian Studies Development Program*.

Dear friend,

I will miss visiting your home in charming *Qingdao*, an old fishing village
first occupied by the Austro-Hungarians who established a brewery
and then by the Japanese who built a tolling station and the railway to *Beijing*.
Today, *Qingdao*, this pearl of a city, remains divided into European and Chinese sections.

You were born in neighboring *Jinan*, where you spent your early years
a hard place of hidden charms and oracle bones
remembered for its ruthless *Red Guard*
daduizhang, young student leaders, and *dazibao*, giant propaganda signs
and *Struggle Meetings*, *Study Groups*, and political prisons for reactionaries.

One day early in our friendship, traveling together on a *Qingdao* bus
we met a VIP, you kindly translating, our conversational go-between.
After that, thanks to your encouragement, I began learning Chinese.

You wanted me to take in all of modern *Qingdao*
beach resort, trading center, aquarium
industrial producer of cars and generators
digital technology, light industry, textiles, and seafood.

Continually with a kind smile, you served as our translator
the only woman leader in the receiving delegation
fierce in your duty, keen in perception.

You warmly introduced me to your friend, Mr. Wang
a regional high official and secret poet
(not unlike *Luo Binwang*, *Tang* Dynasty imperial administrator and poet)
who during my group's first official bus tour of *Qingdao*
honored us with his presence.
Sitting next to you and in front of me, with your patient translations
he talked of works by the revered *Tang* poet *Du Mu*
and by *Lu Xun* and *Ding Ling*, modern authors and literary critics.
Your assistance allowed us to discuss China's long history of f*eng shui*.

Our special bus drove past a park and up a tall hill
where we stopped to visit a huge pagoda, taking lots of pictures.
After that, the bus took us to a vanguard vineyard, to enjoy drinking wine.
You and I connected on some invisible vibratory level.

Sweet Sally,

After that first journey
you invited me to return to *Qingdao* whenever I could.
I arranged trips to China for 6 more summers
and in 1996 you studied economics and policy at the *East-West Center*.

At each subsequent visit, you were my magic charm
the coordinator for my time in *Qingdao*.
You taught me tea civilization, proper relations, and etiquette.
Each time I returned, you reconnected us with Mr. Wang
often at the *Tiange* tea house on a tree-lined street in *Badaguan*
nestled by the sea, a favorite cadre playground
for rest, recuperation, and top-level meetings
in well-preserved mansions, villas, and guest houses.
The 3 of us stumbled across the culture and language divide.

At the tea house, never intrusive, the *fuwuyuan* servers
would flawlessly pour king's tea
from an elegant pot with a meter-long spout
into our small porcelain dragon cups
keeping them continuously full during hours of conversation
while our *dharma* hearts filled with fond and intimate memories.

Sally, I remember that first trip beyond the city
when we drove north to the sacred temple in *Laoshan*
up the mountain from the coast near *Shi Lao Ren*, a stone island off the shore.
In the parking lot, from a vendor selling souvenirs, I bought opal drop earrings.

Walking up the steep path to the *dao* temple, we saw
green crystal-bead curtains sparkling in the light at the entrance.
We heard bells tinkling bells and monks chanting. We smelled incense.
In the Pavilion of Purification, our group was received by the holy man
who graciously granted us an audience and his sacred attention.

Afterwards, I walked alone down a shaded path
to a garden of ancient conifers.
Looking up at the muted blue sky, I glimpsed familiar pine branches
then spotted a huge white flower on a tall magnolia tree.
How had it gotten there?
Did it fly from my childhood back yard in Alabama?
Was it magic, a hallucination?
I longed to smell that ethereal flower's fragrance, wear it in my bushy hair.

Unexpectedly, the holy man was there, slightly behind me.
I felt his strong presence, compassionate.
Intuiting my desire, he picked the blossom, gifting it to me.

Standing there in my purple floppy straw hat
I held the flower in my lotus palms, marveling at a feeling of peaceful joy.
Someone in our group snapped a picture. When I saw it later,
the flower seemed to be floating just above the cradle of my hands
surrounded by an aura of pure white light, opalesque.

From that magnolia moment on, after my first visit
I became obsessed with the holy mountain and *Laoshan*.
I wanted to return, stay at the lamasery, and I wrote you my wish.
You replied it was not possible at that time. Women were unwelcome.
The monastery was an exclusively male sphere of influence.
You, Sally, and other friends
helped me ritually stop at the *Laoshan* district at least once each visit.

Thanks to your *guanxi* we were guests at the mayor's house
feasted on endless exceptionally delicious dishes
spent the night comfortably, woke early, visited the quarry, and bought jade sculptures.

We visited the fishermen, who were repairing their nets spread out on the beach
and we toured a small packing company nearby. People were kind and deferential.
I marveled at the sturdy old wooden boats
learned how seeding the nets produced abundant and varied crustaceans
how the miracles of refrigeration and air travel shared the delicious seafood far and wide.

You introduced me to your family: daughter, mother, sisters, cousins, nieces
your friends in business, the arts, the government, the university.
On rare occasions near the end of your life, we discussed government and politics
the devastation, betrayals, and rewards of the *Cultural Revolution*
contemporary international relations and China's progression into the future.

Part II

Darling Sally, your *guanxi* was amazing!

You arranged for me to tutor English bi-weekly to your friend
a businessman who worked for a big Japanese company
the husband of your good friend who was often away doing business in Korea
because you wanted him to have something constructive to do in her absence.
I was already teaching classes in 2 locations
but the money was good, so I accepted the challenge!

You introduced me, an exotic American Other, to your colleagues.
Being your friend made me an honorary *red princess*.
Your guanxi helped me give lectures to large English classes.
and to a small group of graduate students at the University of *Qingdao*.
Each new visit, I taught ethnic literature, Black history, and poetry.

You listened to me talk about my yearning to meet African students
how I missed seeing Black faces at markets, streets, beaches, and banks.

Another summer, your well-placed friends
hired me to teach conversational English at Holmes College
where about half of my 30-plus students, mid-level businessmen
would be going to Zambia as administrators for a Chinese textile factory.
They were solicitous to their *laoshi* professor
brought me to meet their families in their homes
invited me to weddings, restaurants and shopping.
They taught me how to buy wisely at the open markets
how to select good fish and melons, and how to cook certain Chinese dishes.

I taught the students some Black culture as well
including eating grits, listening to my home music
and dancing, which they all tried and many enjoyed—
but they certainly did not like eating steak and big pieces of meat.

Sally, when I first came to *Qingdao*
the transportation consisted mainly of buses and bikes
and assorted trucks, taxis, wagons, palanquins, and carts.
I rode with you in the handful of government-issued chauffeured cars
trusting you and the drivers, ensconced behind curtains
going to fashionable restaurants and privileged corners
to eat sumptuous meals of 12-20 courses and drink delightful *Tsingtao* beer.
Within a few years, enormous traffic jams filled the city.

Year after year, you generously hosted me for amazing meals
including private-room parties held in the back of upscale restaurants
endless courses of meats, seafood, vegetables, and noodles
cases of beer, a rare bottle of wine, and Chinese *jiou*.
Each room had *karaoke*. Everyone had to sing. Laughter was loud and boisterous.
What adventures we shared—you always a pioneer, a vanguard woman warrior.
I imagine you probably shone even when you were in the *Red Guard*
and participated in *Summer Labor*, led *Study Groups* and *Struggle Meetings*.

Another year, you got your first car and learned to drive!
The first woman in the city?
I confess I was terrified when you drove heedlessly in the wrong direction
down dark 1-way streets on our way home from someplace noteworthy and fancy.

Another special day, on our way to the *Laoshan* district
I remember I was unsettled when you stopped unexpectedly
leaving the car in the middle lane of an almost-empty freeway under construction.
You walked in compact heels all the way across to the other side
to ask directions from a man on a bike cart.
I can see now his load piled precariously high
with secondhand throwaways and broken items
likely to sell after work by the side of the road.

Each year I visited, there were new streets, roads, lanes
the old ones broken up with picks and shovels
by young country workers with strong backs
and a burning desire to make money for the folks back home.
The old streets were continually replaced by larger ones, then came freeways
to accommodate more cars, more drivers, and new housing developments.
Your driving improved with the roads and experience.
Fearless and strong, you never gave up.

Sally, you were full of surprises!
Imagine my going to a golf course in China
when I had never even gone to one in the United States.
You had yet another government-issued car and drove me around.
We took the newest expressway on the way to the country club.
You showed me the housing divisions under construction
boldly cut out of stone mountains or strewn across farmlands.

Fishermen were displaced, whole villages made obsolete
replaced by luxurious, if sometimes poorly constructed
condos and villas overlooking the mountains or the sea.
Years later, fully 1/2 of them remained unoccupied
owned by the wealthy and business speculators
used for weekend retreats and extracurricular activities.

One night, we shared a magical, musical circus-theatre performance
together with your dear friends, powerful Party women in *Qingdao*
Mrs. Z, head of foreign affairs, and Mrs. L, head of culture and arts.
Another evening we went to an unforgettably fabulous fashion show
the models tall and lithe, perfectly coiffed and made-up
the outfits as sophisticated as for fashion week in Paris or New York.

Through the years, I saw your various fine workplaces
such as your office on the 12th floor of City Hall, overlooking the sea
and later your *Shandong* Province governmental office
where you oversaw taxation of foreign corporations
notoriously difficult since they cleverly avoided paying and you had to pursue them.

At the seaside park just across from your office, we strolled around the artworks
in the foggy *Qingdao* evenings with your friend Mrs. H.
I marveled at a towering red iconic conical-layered sculpture 4-stories tall
a shocking abstraction named May Wind
built to honor May Day located in what became known as May *4th Square*.
The 20-foot tall piano sculpture nearby was a surprise
mechanically playing scheduled classical concerts, filling the park with music.

We rarely went to the museum or any of the 6 bathing beaches in *Qingdao*
or to *Golden Beach*, *Huangdao*, on the island nearby across the bay
but sometimes we ate lunch where we could see and enjoy the seaside beauty.

To relax and enjoy the outdoors
we went on walks in *Zhongshan* Park and admired the flowers
visited *Zhanqiao* Pavilion and strolled in the park by Fushan Bay
took small excursions on weekends, and in the evening before the 9 p.m. curfew.

Most of all, I remember our famous lunches
at hotels, restaurants, tea houses, and the university—you changed my palate!

You always made time to take me on my favorite activity, shopping
driving me to an upscale mall, a prestigious dressmaker, and open markets
where prices were more affordable
where I got shoes from a street cobbler
where I purchased perfume from the essential-oil man
where one could buy birds, *bonsai* trees, poultry, and more
where I found the fine antique porcelain that decorates my home.

Early on, you introduced me to your beloved daughter, Mang Mang.
I watched her grow into a young woman
traveling to study journalism and languages in Japan and the U.S.
She and her friends thoughtfully took me to stores and restaurants.
Both alike and different from you, she loved diversity and languages
a technology savvy non-conformist appreciative of the fine things in life.
After fearing she would never marry
you happily got to meet her American fiancé who became her husband.

It was she who wrote and told me of your death.

Part III

I will never forget the day you took me to yet another special event:
the massive celebrations for the opening of a new industrial-zone city!

Before our motorcade departed from *Lancun* City Hall, a tea server provided
the customary 3 cups of tea for officials and guests, with peaches and cherries.
We rode in a caravan of black government cars with red flags on the hood
carrying important government officials, dignitaries, and *moi*!
You were up front in another car with the mayor.
I was your personal guest in the last chauffeured black sedan.

I was befuddled by the Chinese language swirling around me
you no longer by my side to interpret.
We hurtled speedily toward the coast for the dedication ceremonies.

We passed quickly by many blocked streets.
The jingcha police had halted all carts, bicycles, trucks, and car traffic.
Standing at attention in their tidy uniforms, they saluted our convoy
while citizens cautiously peeped out from behind the lines
to see who was creating such an inconvenience.

We whizzed beyond the city limits
through the flat countryside to our destination.
The whole new town dressed in matching orange hats and t-shirts
was waiting patiently for us to arrive and the event to begin
at the outdoor venue featuring 4 sections, each with 500 folding chairs.

You were on stage with the *Shandong* officials and dignitaries.
I was privileged to sit with distinguished guests in the second row.
and honored when they recognized me, calling my name and asking me to stand.
I was your special African American guest from *Hawai`i*
presented with a matching shirt and cap with the town's name, which I still have.

Meanwhile, I fantasized about doing business in China
selling silk, leather, embroidery, jade, stone sculptures, shell art, clothes, shoes
products available through your friends, relatives, and their businesses.
After you took me to the many factories in that special economic zone
where delegations supplied tea, fruits, lavish dinners, and endless drinks
and talk of joint ventures proliferated, I imagined attainment of financial success.

I returned home to *Hawai`i* and spoke of my dreams
but a professor and poet, I did not get financial backing in the U.S. Alas!

When I visited, you or another friend greeted me at the train station or airport.
Each year, I met more of your family and colleagues.
We took tours and excursions in and around *Qingdao*.
Often, we rode chauffeured by your driver or by Mr. L
director of a hi-tech park, who would become a TV personality.

Later, he came to *Hawai`i*, part of an official delegation
visited me bearing gifts: beautiful Chinese scrolls with poems on each one.
I have them around the house, and in my studio/office where you spent the night.
After that, by the lake at *Beihai* Park in *Beijing*, I met his daughter and her *fiancé*
learning about her fantastic media job with the *Xinhua* News Agency.

Sally, you made me strong!

You opened your 3-bedroom government-appointed condo to me
(a sign of your excellent work, you received it long before others did).
On *Dong Hai* Road, it was a 3-story penthouse
with an elevator and a view down the hill of the harbor.
For 2 of the 7 summers I spent in China, I stayed on the 8th floor
of a dormitory for foreign teachers. No elevator there—wow!
But for the other 5 summers you insisted that I stay in your penthouse
bigheartedly giving me first the whole 2nd floor and later the entire 3rd floor.

Daily, I loved slipping through your window, stepping out onto your roof
drinking special harvest tea and observing the people and traffic below
who came and went noisily, colorfully, industriously, stylishly.
I observed patterns of activities, getting to know the neighborhood from up high.

I burned incense bought at the temple
filled the rooms with fresh flowers
spread out my crystals, inspirational books, pictures, and recent purchases
covered the chairs with my brightly designed *pareo* and wrote poems.

You did not always approve of my unconventional
and sometimes common *Qingdao* friends who liked to party
yet you never complained about my style or artistic endeavors
but rather admired my independence, fierce like yours.
We had daily English lessons to practice your pronunciation.
Sometimes, in the early mornings you joined me on the roof
as you read English-language magazines and newspapers.

China finally opened, permitting its citizens to travel abroad
but before then you went on government-sponsored delegations
mostly with men, opening the path, setting the pace
a tough woman out front checking major corporations
Chicago, San Francisco, New York
Paris, Rome, Johannesburg, Prague
Calcutta, Durban, Rio de Janeiro, the Philippines, Dubai, and more.

You delighted in travel, other languages, cultures, and foreigners
bought fancy designer scarves, shoes, purses, gloves, watches
from all over the world and in China, and shared some with me.

Did so much travel lower your immune system?
Did exhaustion make you susceptible to the fatal disease?
You called me sometimes on the telephone to talk
distressed. Your English seemed worse, and my Chinese skills were fading.

It was my last visit, and you were ill, but you still met me at the train station
thin, chilled, looking tired, with a warm smile on your face.
You confessed you had been to doctors in *Beijing, Shanghai*, and of course *Qingdao*.
You had tried the best traditional Chinese medicine and Western medicine.
There was no diagnosis, or did you just not tell me?
Your color changed. You became jaundiced, had stomach pain
could no longer enjoy going out to eat those lavish and delicious
16-course dinners abundant in fabulous *Qingdao*.
Was it pancreatitis?

I was surprised when your meimei, younger sister, arrived from *Jinan*
helped cook and care for you.
I began to understand the utter gravity of your health condition.
One day, she took a break and went to the mountain village in *Laoshan*
with me and my friends to pick apricots, eat with the farmers.
We had so much fun and laughed the whole day.
I wished you could have been there too.

Another time, you left me with your older sister, your *jiejie*
who cared for her son's children
in a tall new apartment building on the *Laoshan* coast.
She and I had made *jiaoze* for the afternoon.
You were weak then, almost too sick to drive
but you took me and left me there. I suspect you went to the doctor.

That night, we returned to your house and I packed.
The next morning
You drove me to the train station.
We said goodbye. I never saw you again.

Sally,
today I listened to the *Chi Lights* croon
"missing you . . . lonely . . . got to move on . . ."
then to *Kathleen Battle* with *Jean-Pierre Rampal*.
I had heard this music while wearing earphones at the *Summer Palace*.
just before meeting you for the first time. Traveling to the east of *Beijing*
we stayed at a Chinese hotel, the *Hua Tian* in *Qingdao*.

Sally,
photos, memories, and words can never capture
your generous and adventuresome spirit
intelligence, tough-minded courage, unwavering determination.
Your sensitivity and perception were a gift
from the night of our first banquet in *Qingdao*
when I danced *hula* for the group
to our last fond farewell some 15 years later.

Sally,
I missed you at the huge tropical birthday party
arranged by my daughters whom you had met, loved, and respected.
It was the perfect gift.
You would have marveled at the flowers and music, delighted in the people.
Born the day after Christmas, I thought about you the whole holiday season
but had been too busy with family, friends, and rituals of loving and sharing
to give you what I later understood would have been our final phone call.

My husband Harvey gave you a drawing of *Charlotte's Web*
a *dharma* riddle. You loved his artwork
wanted to buy and sell it in China, another project unfulfilled forever.

A wave ripples out and touches many lives.
You were the polished jade stone that made the waves
touched my essence, shared, and made me love your city.
I always wanted a place to live in or near *Qingdao*.
My friend Ruth, a psychic, said of our past lives
that my husband and I had been farmers by the *South China Sea*.
I think of farmlands south of *Qingdao*.
After my 3rd summer in China, I reread her intuitive words.
No wonder I felt so at home in *Qingdao*.

Dear Sally,
I have to write out my grief to understand its meaning.
I have so much admiration, respect, and soaring gratitude for you.
We shared courage, laughter, adventure, independence, and unspoken love.
For you, I write this tribute.
I miss you so much. Forever love from your friend, Kathryn.

DISAPPEARANCES

Where flows the smile of contentment
when all we cherish disappears like migrating birds
on the northern lawn of morning's dream?

Where goes the southern hug of spring
when those we love evaporate like steam
from a fresh-cooked favorite dish?

Where glides the soft and perfect skin of summer
the easy movement of laughter, the light of hope?
Where settles the harvest of Western wisdom and Eastern understanding
when winter dims the sight, and sucks the sounds away?

Why try to succeed
when we see ourselves
fade into a mere trace
of infinite possibilities and unfamiliar space?
We find ourselves wingless at the Yellow Crane Pavilion
shimmering dust on a dim and polluted path to heaven.
Why try again?

A few chosen treasures
in contextual memories
pebbles and pearls—
is that all we have?

PAINFUL SEPARATION

In the afternoons, following classes
at 4:30, the university PA plays
approved music to end the workday.
Songs blast every corner, crack, and
crevice throughout the campus.
A daily favorite is *Whitney Houston*
who repeats in reassurance
"I'll always love you."

Each hour, minute, second seems long
every meal, banquet, farewell occasion
painful already, even before I leave.
"Let me say I'll miss you" colors
each rose sunrise, vermillion sunset.
Crimson tears I silently shed
from my heart overflowing
each moonrise, star shine, moonset.

I only wish
I knew more *Zhongwen*, words to speak
learned more nuances of your character
your culture and favorite colors.
I can hardly wait to return again
to see you, know you more.
I picture you in my mind
smiling so sincerely
richer today than yesterday in my soul.
I want to give you my joy and satisfaction.
I want to feel you close like the wind.
I fly so far away, too soon to imagine.
Tomorrow's separation closes in like
winter.

Absence threatens an untended dwelling.
Let me say once more
"I'll always love you."
My love is predictable
like wedding dresses in China
yet reliable as the sun in *Hawai`i*.
I enjoy the way that you
conservative and understated
love me steadily and strongly.
"I need you before I leave you."
You look my way.
I call your name.
I look to you and take flight.

Summer fog and foreignness
obfuscates my bright blue emotions
I hold on to a moonlit dream.
We will always be connected.
The poetry of *Li Shangyin* stirs
spectral themes of loss and parting.

"Let me say once more I love you."
I leave in sadness, my departure inevitable
But for those we love
it is enough to remember
to capture the fleeting sensation of joy
unforgettable hope
of another tomorrow.
Phantom possibilities.

HEAT WAVE AT MIDNIGHT

A small timid breeze
tries to enter my flat at midnight
nudging gently.

But it quickly retreats
from the dragon of heat within.

I toss and turn
but cannot sleep
you still stirring in my mind
a friendly poltergeist.

V

OPAL MOON SHADOWS

Lotus Traditions and Generations

BELL CULTURE

At daybreak, ancestral bronze bells
toll culture and history and antiquity
through the stone walls of China
authentic sounds, forgotten sacred songs.

Big brass bells at temples for cultural rituals
call to the world, unwritten worship
in clear shining tones
while nearby musicians
play *erhu* fiddles and bamboo flutes
a blaze of sun lighting poetic words
of venerable *Wu Chengen*
on my heart's page of imagined dramas
and energetic performers.

Bell tones in the DNA, in the voice
clanging pots and flatware in the kitchen
cymbals, singers, storytellers, visionaries
amid generations of classical remembrance
talking traditions, morality plays
ballad singers, pageants, Chinese opera
communication bowls and legends of bells.

Brass strength of families and ancestors
withstanding withering time
bells arouse the masses, call children home.
Symbols of power and elliptical survival

imperial court bells sound in the 3rd eye.
A troubadour serenades nacre emotions
under a *bodhi* tree on a wet holiday
as bicycle bells ring out.

Tiny bells and distant temple chants mingle
in silent ribbons of morning mist
soft as silk in the garden of lingering dawn.
Tender pine breeze carries sustainable
memory of sacred sounds.

Ancient bells tear the air
and sound the night watch
awaken uncertain dreams, sacrificial rites.
Complex tones of bell sizes, shapes, and
materials announce events.

Bells and chimes connect communities
mark offerings to ancestors and spirits
recall ceremonies and dances
portrayed in theatrical performances
inspiring awe in the ghosts and the gods.
Bells, cymbals, drums, and *pipa* lutes follow
a traditional wedding ceremony.

****

Afterwards, the poet sits in a remote town
reflects alone on a kang bed, writes of
the *4 Directions* and *5 Elements* of *feng shui*
each requiring ritual bells
of a different size and tone
rhymes ringing true, rain ringing bells
venerable bells commanding
attention and reverence.

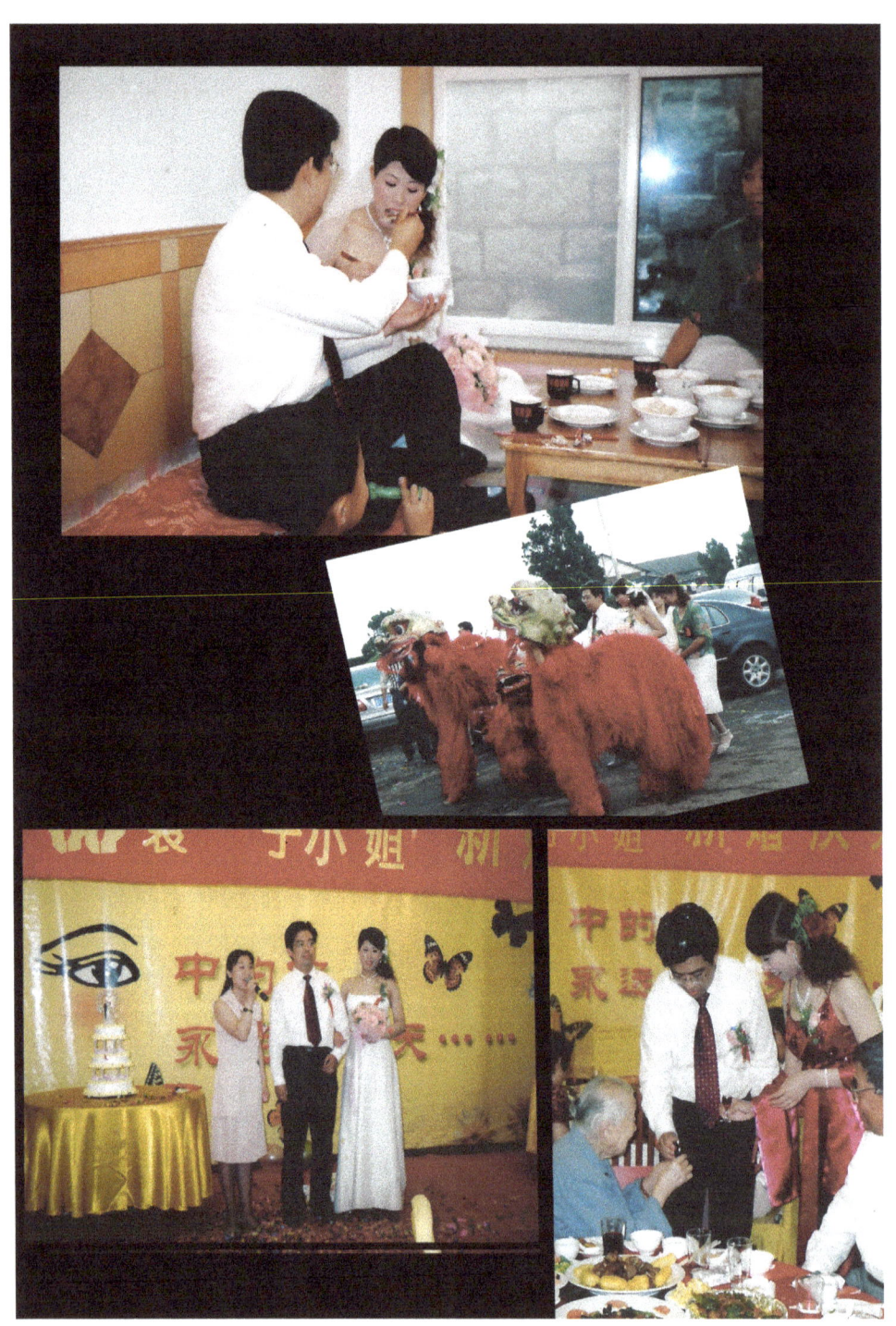

GATES OF CHINA

Dragon Gates of stone and earth, metal and wood, separate and protect
the *hutong*, the community, the university
the modern compound for foreigners
the slate workers' unit
the hungry illegal migrants' hidden tents.
The walls and gates of the city
anchor the red-flag country
separate China from outsiders and invasions.

Dragon Gate, Phoenix Gate, and innumerable named others
flourish in every city, town, hamlet, community
maintained and sustained over generations.

Gates mark the 4 directions: *donghuamen, xihuamen, shenwumen, beihuamen*
ceremonial archways and architectural structures.
carved, rectangular, round, painted, wood, stone gates
arched mythological barriers against strangers, enemies, criminals, invaders
gates with dragons and lions for protection against lost evil spirits
gates with frogs for abundance and water
a golden circle gate for survival
bamboo gates for flexible longevity.
All reflect the legendary *5 Virtues* in people's customary minds.

Inside a city, inner gates to communities
inside communities, walls within gates
crimson gates, elaborate beams
gates resting on pillars or stone, covered with colorful tiles
gates to hidden pavilions
gates to separate small homes in a *hutong*
the perennially crowded community gardens of families and neighbors.

I pass through my favorite, a round moon-gate where 3 scholar's stones
and a stand of bamboo (legendary friend in winter and summer)
welcome friends to read *Li Bai* and *Su Shi*
to discuss *dao* poets *Li Qingzhao, Lady Xu Mu*, and *Wang Wei*.
They take tea, drink wine, and relax for unscripted hours
within the time-honored protection and privacy of gates and walls.

AT THE PEARL MOON PAVILION

A woman ponders the *lotus* flowers in a small pond
at the Water Moon veranda of the Pearl Moon Pavilion.

The resplendent opal moon
makes her nightly lucent tour
over the woman in the great garden of Glorious Felicity.
Floating cloud-gauze dances above
changing shadows with the whims of the summer breeze.

The palace of the Moon Queen reigns high over the earth's night.
Her radiant beauty reflects in milky moonbeams
casting a spell over the temple of the earth.
Her glow adorns the woman's sepia skin.

The magic of the evening
belies the chaos in the city and feelings of unrequited love
evoking the memory of lost pleasures in the lyrical poems of *Li Yu*.

Restless, the woman walks on in the huge garden.
She pauses on the glowing white bridge
full of celestial longing
on the moonlit hillside.
Shadows shift.

Fueled by the mirth of starlight, clouds, and moon
the woman's pewter passion of dissatisfaction dissolves.
Her small smile complements the ghostly pearl moonlight
dancing impersonally over the troubled world.

THE *GREAT WALL*

To be above an ancient town at a more remote section of the *Great Wall*
surrounded by apple and almond groves
seeing from on high the silvered sliver of a running stream
and chives, watermelon, and wheat sweltering under a tall lid of slate sky
was exhilarating!

We moved higher on the wall
beyond multiple generations in small groups
chattering Chinese tourists overpowering the space
past the monotonous chirping of *maque* sparrows and *banqiu* crickets
into deep folds of the tall hills.
Youths quickly overtook us.

The Chinese tourists climbed easily
a few women in skirts, stockings, and heels
remarkably strong people moving forward and up
while we Americans huffed and puffed up the heights.

Members of our group took different directions.
A friend did *taiji* on the ledge
above where I sat alone in rarified air
waiting for silence and stillness to return.
I baked like a lizard nestled in a nook of lichen-covered rocks.

Enormous blue ants scrambled away from the path of passing people.
A fluttering monarch butterfly sought honey
from the fragrance of nearby tiny pink flowers.
Ochre butterflies escaped the strong shadows all around, bursting in freedom.
Buzzing honeybees and singing sparrows slipped
through the screened curtain of voices
while thorny bushes confirmed the treacherous passes beyond.
Rolling hills sheltered a copse of emerald poplars and a hidden ancestral shrine.

A small plane passed like a pesky intruder
the intensifying sun and heat belying the calm façade of the day
menacing red thunder approaching, shaking the earth.

The unusual chameleon sky announced a surprise summer storm.
Clouds gathered quickly, seemed to weigh heavy as large stones
portending the full moon deluge that was sure to follow.
An uneasy stillness settled around me
until I was swallowed once again by more youthful tourists
who chattered like the mockingbirds in the nearby trees.

I felt far away from all those I love
yet full of *Guan Yin*'s compassionate spirit of peace and joy.

I moved farther away from the main path
as groups rushed by to find shelter in nearby transportation.
Sounds fell quieter.

While butterflies darted
black-and-white thoughts drifted away like leaves or petals
lagged behind flying feelings.
As curious insects visited on my clothes
and the motor of a bright-yellow truck far below echoed in passing
a distant horn signaling its departure
I prepared to make my steep way down the wall, joining the others.

Feeling out of pattern and free from familiarity
people shared complicated personal stories
spoke of politics, diplomatic intrigues, ancestors, and ill-fated love affairs.
I walked slowly and digested new thoughts
at this lonely section of the wall rolling to the horizon.

A final glimpse unfolded in the distance
recalling legends of *Qin Shi Huangdi*, unifier of China, visionary builder of the *Great Wall*.

RETREAT AT THE SUMMER PALACE

Anyone could spend more than a lifetime deluded at *Yiheyuan*, the *Summer Palace*
forgetting to return home
leaving behind news about the turbulence of terror
disappearing into the seductive royal gardens
listening to conversations of orioles and crickets around Lake *Kunming*.

At the intersection of the lake and the covered walkway's edge
a many-ton marble dragon boat rests immobile
sunk into the water, too heavy to move
battling the mud of the lake through the seasons in its splendid carved glory.

The elegant grand Hall of Benevolence and Longevity
bestows an aura of harmony and well-being
almost makes one forget humanity's perennial plight of ego:
international intrigues, diplomatic *faux pas*, brutal battles, scorching wars
intolerance of differences, lack of compassion, and savagery
the poisonous ravaging of species in our shared home, the enduring body of the Earth.

At this serene retreat
visitors ride on a small peaceful dragon boat
to see the island of a notable concubine
who organized retreats for writers and artists
in the ornate pavilions and verdant courtyards generations ago.

While crossing the tall arch of the stone bridge
       visitors stop
       breath stunned by the jade beauty of this place.
I could spend 10,000 mornings
       sitting on a different sitting stone each day of a lifetime
       meditating and watching the passing clouds.
I could spend 12 years
regarding a different statue each evening
examining one of 17,000 drawings across the long covered corridor
entertaining guests or children with the numerous painted mythical tales.

The alluring green spaces and healing *feng shui* of the *Summer Palace*
teach visitors to return to our lives with humility, gratitude, and love for the earth.

IMPERIAL STEPS AND STONES

Steep stone steps over monumental rocks impress.
Thick slabs lead up to the Great Hall and Pavilion of Peace and Harmony
where one views the distance and landings that oversee
the great artificial lake and ornamental grounds.

Confucian discipline for the young builders who died daily
cutting and moving giant thick slabs of granite stones
intentional placing of heavy, up-down times
years working at the great monument to nobility
steps wide enough for a row of 6 to ascend side by side.

Up up up! I climb slowly the hard steps
each stone at least 100 times my weight.
Perspective changes, more objective from above
and a sense of awe and admiration overwhelms.
Tired, I rest on an elevated veranda
watch a giant black-and-white magpie glide by
surveying sweeping quickly the pavilion's ornate 3-tiered, blue-tiled roof
pausing for a bit in some gnarled pine branches
before flying over a nearby aspen tree.
It settles on a tall stone ledge facing the placid Lake *Kunming*.
just beyond my line of vision.

Here among the tourists
ironically near the Pavilion of Exalted Felicity
I feel my foreignness, the dark outsider
an ornamental presence, exotic, disposable
fragile like a beautifully painted porcelain vase
unique and unnecessary.

Gardens of myriad trees
decorative art on gates, doors, bells, furniture, temples, pagodas
creativity's epiphanies and paradoxes
adornment in all directions from my fragmented perspective
pathways of inspiration for poets like *Tao Qian* and *Ban Jeyiu*—
wherever one turns in the panorama of grandeur
Nature surprises.

Steps to higher and lower perceptions
remnants of gnarled centuries, conflicted generations
smoothed by the intentional beauty
created for the retreat into a protected haven of pleasures
forgiving of power-driven history and dramas of dominance
the timeless aesthetic setting/experience of the *Summer Palace* heals like tea.

* * * * * * * * * * *

Back in *Beijing* after dinner at *Beida*
I walk up other steps, practical and wooden
to the tiny slightly drab dorm rooms, each with 6 *chuang* beds and 4 desks
into the room of my new friends
African foreign students on scholarships, soon-to-be diplomats.

I learn that Chinese-American relations
have been falling apart since morning, boundaries blurred
ambassadors/envoys threatened to be recalled.

I tell them laughing
"In case of an international incident, *qing*, please, take me to write
behind the walls at the inspirational sumptuous *Summer Palace*
send me up the indestructible Imperial steps and stones
leave me hidden on a small island of forever
far from *CCTV* until the fiery hostilities are resolved."

AT QUFU, HOME OF CONFUCIUS

Friendly trees greet the visitors to *Qufu*
birthplace of the great master *Confucius*.
The stately campus of *Qufu* Teachers' College
is a fitting legacy to the great educator.
To trade knowledge and his love of learning
for a faithful following of students
he marketed traditions of decorum, moderation, humility
the rewarding breeze of honor and respect
seeds of principles of virtue, honesty, listening, and compassion
providing rich soil for young generations of scholars, poets
the *Tao Te Ching*.

Dedication to others made him a testament
of a person's psychological intellectual and moral possibilities.
Philosopher King at the Round Pavilion
Confucius was virtuous, a black dragon of fearless seeking and teaching
his ideas of excellence for leaders evolving, elevating, everlasting
his light and knowledge sustaining leaders, students, the far-flung masses
his practice: love the people, be humble, be the words.

Sitting at his gravesite, I imagine *Confucius*
the lightning of his teachings bright and bold steles, communication tradition.
He made dark clouds of ignorance dissipate with knowledge.
His precepts about dignity traveled the country.
His wise teachings in the Garden of Fecundity influenced generations.
His daring challenge of transformation inspired his followers.
Today, the sun soars in the sky over antiquity at *Qufu*.

REVELATION AT MOUNT TAI

Taishan is the mythological home of the *Dawn Cloud Sovereign*.
His daughter, the merciful *Guan Yin*, known as *Goddess of Compassion*
shares his mountain realm, an alleged sacred source of healings and blessings.

An arduous pilgrimage to Marvel Peak requires climbing 5,000 stairs
up the tall shoulder of the inspirational height.
A soft morning glow, almost invisible, paints the dawn
and a holiday breeze traverses the rugged beauty of the golden landscape.
A bald eagle circles high overhead, a favored early morning omen
weaving a *mandala* of hope amid the incredible crags of betrayal.
Some say *Taishan* is the legendary *Mount Meru*, consecrated center of the universe.

The clouds lift and open up the vista over the Sky Tasting Pavilion—
a controversial new wing with an inner garden and steep cliffs
reveals the recovered rock sculpture from the *Song* Dynasty
long ago stolen from the royal sacred retreat at *Taishan*
bandits hoodwinked into selling precious historical artifacts for financial gain.

Millions of visitors each month
climb to seek forgiveness and answers to longings, passions
imprint the feeling and magical scene on the quivering soul of their being.

This morning, high on the revered mountain bluffs, births a string of jade moments
intimate, tranquil, unforgettable, inconsequential and almost invisible
I pass by the panorama of sacred splendor
stop to rest and drink tea from my thermos
savor some stillness at the Pavilion of Emerald Heights.

A wooden *phoenix* resting on a sculpted perch near a *parasol tree* catches my attention.
My inner garden shifts with each new direction.
The *5-Crest Mountains* invite other worldly apparitions and ghosts
beckon pilgrims and tourists to go higher to the frightful cliffs of human life.
Within or without a tangible frame, I heed the shivering call toward the golden peak.

Perceptions and panorama change with the ribbons of early pearly mists.
Nearby at the Pagoda of Ample Blessings, a huge brass censer sends soporific smoke
pungent clouds of temple incense covering and protecting the steep, rocky passage.
Alongside, jasmine blossoms waft sweetness and encourage gratitude.
The pilgrims who struggle up and down the revered mountain experience wholeness.
I remember compassionate *Guan Yin* and take heart.

We are all strewn in imperfection on strings of irregular prayer beads
travelers on the worn paths up and down sacred *Taishan*, seeking blessings and forgiveness.

BEIDA (*PEKING* UNIVERSITY)

Beida, like a stunning woman of a certain age
witness to classical education, historical knowledge
countless great love affairs of notable people
heroic dramas and revolutionary intrigue
in spite of peeling paint and 1990s neglect is beautiful!

Still holding its colonial name, *Peking* University, but known to Chinese as *Beida*
since 1898 has educated the brilliant elite from provinces near and far.
It features 3- and 4-story walkups in traditional Chinese design
showcase of durable structures graced by classic lines
colorful eaves, covered painted walkways
soft gardens, giant antique hand-painted vases.
Stone monsters and armed guards greet all
at the wide welcoming entrances to campus.
pathways with carved stone bridges
meander around manmade streams and lakes
with noble rock gardens hidden by artificial mounds and hillocks.
Grass hand cut with sickles or even uncut
softens the dilapidated surfaces of enduring elegance.

Daily at dawn
I sit protected at the Pear Tree Pavilion
where mists soften the general disrepair
and poor lighting camouflages the unkempt walls and hallways
products of government oversight and misplaced priorities
proof of the illegitimate practices of some corrupted officials.

I face the *lotus* Pond of Heavenly Branches
watch a slow procession of miniature frogs
make their way across a stone bridge in the north corner
instinctively avoiding large prey.
Above the eaves of the *pavilion*
swallows and bats in their frenetic dance dart
distinctive black flashes against the lightening pastel sky
which at sunrise unveils the mammoth city of *Beijng*.

Nearby I hear coughing, spitting, then stillness at *Beida*
as people go within for a short time to find a peaceful center
early light camouflaging men and women of all ages.
People practice *taiji* or swords to strengthen the core and brighten the vision
against the unsettling movements of 20-million *hoi polloi*
officials, office and factory workers, entrepreneurs, and foreign investors.

All compete for survival. A brass bell rings. Students rush to classes and promise at *Beida*.

STILLNESS AND MOVEMENT

I return again to *Beida* in summer
an intellectual oasis in a bustling *Beijing*
on a late Sunday morning. No classes.

I sit and idle by the lake.
A white butterfly darts gracefully.
A child's laughter tinkles in the heavy gray air.
3 glistening ducks fly in and land noisily on the jade lake.
Chattering swallows dart like arrows to and from their still nests
hidden under ornately carved beams
artfully designed and painted bold reds, greens, and peacock blues.

Families pass steadily around the green lake
talking noisily, predictable as a summer shower.
Solitary ones sit still like statues
listening, reflecting, observing.
Small fish ripple the surface, jump, fall
make magic circles extending like *mandala* into the maze of history.

Here and there colonies of yellow water lilies
fringe the hem of the lake like lace
presence in stillness.
You, dear one, are far away
yet your memory moves in my heart
bright as the spring sun behind the clouds lighting my day.

Beida is still a stunning pearl
more students, professors, *waiguo* foreigners, locals, groundskeepers
new modern buildings squeezed between classical structures
covered passageways and well-tended gardens welcoming the throngs.

I walk around, a lone Black foreigner
hands clasped behind my back Chinese-style
going past the familiar Sun Gate Pavilion
silent witness to generations of secrets
complex rebellions and surreptitious romances.
I pause and brood over conflicts.

Over there, across the campus road
beyond the traffic jam of Audis, Lexuses, taxis, and luxury sedans
tennis players wait patiently for open courts
in front of the remodeled 4-star guest house
host to international scholars and conferences
rooms no longer dingy, dark, and gray.

The luxuriant jade lake remains enigmatic
perennial *chi* of the university flowing predictably to survival
mirroring passing pedestrians, *pengyou* who playfully whisper.
An ornate dragon bridge arches picturesque beside the weeping willows.
All around movement stirs the heavy air.

Hidden pathways threading through shade trees
lead to public gardens and quiet retreats where
elders still practice *taiji* at sunrise
radical youths still secretly scheme
lovers still furtively embrace
children still play hide and seek in the gardens
students still learn
studying the classics of *Confucius* and Chinese heroes
as well as political philosophy and international relations
math, science, technology, and engineering.

Rich history is born, politics change, and traditions are preserved at *Beida*.

HIDDEN SPLENDOR

At the 4-tiered pagoda
In an abandoned rock garden
Peach tree leaves shadow dance and enchant on the cracked cement pavement below.

Unfamiliar swallows joyfully flit and hide above in colorful Chinese rafters nearby.
Honeybees buzz and move intuitively to taste purple nectars.
Morning delights the unconscious souls of the jasmine blossom nymphs.

Orange and white butterflies flutter. Large bluebirds and magpies seemingly
Observe the writer sitting next to the sculpture of poet *Du Fu*.
All share a space of silence and natural noises in the overgrown rock garden.

A ragged hedge of mock orange blossoms
Leads to the Round Pavilion
Where fragrance wafts along untended rock pathways.

A 12-foot-tall stone sculpture
Sits in the middle of a dirty, green jasper pool
Filled with weeds, neglect, and a dead toad.

Surprise: 8 crimson *lotus* flowers
Bloom bodaciously, another promise from the mud
Nature's bounty hidden from easy view.

FRAGRANCE IN MOONLIGHT

The fog appears like a lover
unspoken and silently familiar
a wraith touching the Chinese city softly like water
penetrating every texture, curve, crevice
with delicate bedtime caresses.
The fog fades late.
The waiting moon appears
and charms the stars and perfumed shadows around midnight.
The dancing patina of silver light on dark skin
complements the fragrance of gardenias, the fog seductive in this poltergeist pleasure garden.

STYMIED IN SUNLIGHT

Summer radiance at the 5-tiered pagoda
perilous exposure to a veiled soul
dare we show ourselves?

Our pampered garden of self lounges at the Pavilion of Green Envy
pale imitation of heaven's ethereal splendor corrupting discovery
why bother with perennial dirt?

Opiates of ghostly emotions and frantic uncertainty
blanket the cities, public policies, government
desiccated possibilities, stymied efforts of regeneration.

Does the 1,000-petaled *lotus* of compassion
predictably bloom in early morning
Does a beautiful dazzle of wheel-flower
ascend from the dark mud, offer the beauty of hope, and wilt in the radiant sun?

YU GARDEN

Yuyuan garden is an oasis in the ancient city of *Shanghai*
a retreat from the throbbing Chinese and French quarters
behind the simple but thick walls of royal dynasties
spaces aesthetically designed in a labyrinth of paths
to give the illusion of an endless garden *mandala*
100s of places to experience in a compact zone
gardens, rooms, *pavilions*, ponds, gazebos, rockeries
for meditation, conversations, persuasions
nooks for forming official strategies and policies
reflection pools where schools of giant golden carp
glisten leisurely then dart like thoughts to other spaces.

A statue of *Guan Yin* seems to feed fish while *lotus* flowers luxuriate
on a bed of emerald leaves near the purple bamboo grove.
More than 400 years of history, intrigue, and court life
permeate and vibrate through this tea house
as throngs of visitors discover the architectural glories
of the *Ming* Dynasty—the carved windows and colorful eaves.

In the chamber of 100,000 flowers, I rest and contemplate the dance
of scattered morning light on a bamboo grove and fan-leafed *gingko* tree.
Miniature grottos, rocks and stones selectively chosen, arranged with care
evoke *qi*, poetry of *Wu Chengen*, and abstract psychological spaces.
Deep in the bamboo stand, I find a room of shade
respite from the relentless summer sun.
Here birds chirp louder than the chattering crowds.
Magnolia trees grace me with a heavenly perfume
contrasting with the sweaty press of persons in the streets outside.
For 100s of generations this *Ming* tea house has hosted receptions
for dynastic officials and international intrigue.
In another small garden are 400 varieties of plants, rare and familiar.

Outside, in front of the traditional wall, sits a guardian dragon
ancient symbol of power and energy, mediator of heaven and earth.
Under his great head and ferocious, fiery strength
sits his companion and friend, the frog
harbinger of rain, water, cleansing, and prosperity.
This unlikely pair of *yin* and *yang* symbols ever remain.

As the sizzling day gives way to promise of a serene evening
the white jade sun transforms into a luminous pearl moon.
Shadows dance to the apogee of the indwelling possible.

FESTIVAL OF LANTERNS

The evening of the Festival of Lanterns
a large crane sits high in a sycamore tree in *Zhongshang* Park
suddenly visible after being hidden by a thick cloud of summer fog
observing the traditional offerings to the ancestors
the purple veils of incense at the Pavilion of Bright Clouds
the flamboyant theatrical entertainment of music, dance, and acrobatics
the parade of ornamental lanterns made of silk, gauze, rice paper, crystal, and glass.

Below a sculptured pathway
adorned with fancy lantern frames and gaudy colors
beautiful shapes of *lotus*, fish, water lilies, and running horses
beckons the children, the mystified and enchanted *waiguo*, and locals.

Nearby, in a hidden cove of the gardens, a story teller enchants the listeners:
a parasol tree tempts the mythical *phoenix* to land
but its imagined flight is to a grove of bamboo
surrounded by embroidered banners.

The crane remains still and detached.
Amid the ceremonial rituals, gaiety, and fireworks extravaganza
in the season of beauty and the *4 Gentlemen of Flowers*
the flower spirits wander invisible under an opal moon
the children run and squeal, chasing the imaginary characters and birds.
All marvel and rejoice at the spectacle of lavish gift-giving and red envelopes
homage and good fun at the annual, much-anticipated Festival of Lanterns, *Yuanxiao*.

TEA, *TAIJI*, AND TRADITION

I

Cool morning fog invites the early riser to abandon fire-fox dreams
to visit rare spirits hidden among the plum and *lotus* blossoms.

3 dragons dance on a white porcelain teacup
forming a patterned circle in gold, blue, and green.

Even on the hottest of days, I enjoy ritualized tea and meditation
appreciating the silent space, while greeting good luck in the morning.

Tea graciously arrives

> before *taiji* circles, pushing, grasping the bird's tail
> before and after meals
> before lovemaking, births, rituals, visitations.

Throughout generations ancient and modern, tea is served

> under auspicious crabapple trees, near lotus ponds
> in new condos, malls, old *pavilions*, in familiar *hutong*
> in small rooms under shadows of towering buildings and cranes.

Following tea and group *taiji* with *pengyou*, dear friends, I open, breathe, expand.

Gathering for news, the national rituals, public announcements
music, and hot *congee* porridge, we set safe travels as our aim.

We embark on an excursion to the *Imperial Summer Palace*
in a modern air-conditioned tour bus
to embrace dynastic history and territory:

> *Qin Shi Huangdi*, who unified China and built the Great Wall
> *Da Yu*, the first emperor to found a hereditary dynasty
> *Puyi*, the final emperor, controlled by his aunt, the *Old Dowager*.

All Chinese honor tea traditions.

II

Upon our arrival at the *Imperial Summer Palace*
we step back to beginnings of Chinese history under a *Beijing* sky
caught by tall, heavy, clouds of summer gray heat.

The scale and grandeur, the balance and symmetry
curved roofs and small fearsome dragons warding off evil spirits
shock and seem to contradict the modern push for materialism and survival.

Our tour guide regales us with Chinese legends about tigers, bears, frogs, and dragons
shares the history of Emperor *Puyi*, the last royal leader of the palace
who tried to be a better man but was controlled and blocked by his authoritative aunt.

We pause and find a quiet place to take tea and practice the 24 *taiji* movements.
An ancient stone courtyard's refreshing coolness eases fatigue, hunger, and excitement.

> A young *gongmin* sits nearby under the shade of a *bodhi*
> watches a woman sip steaming tea at the nearby Peace Pavilion
> rests immobile for many minutes in the enchanting shadows of the mythical tree.

After 3 cups of hot tea, we finally take our main tour:

> gates and walkways
> archaic *pavilions* and halls
> dragon and camel-hump bridges.

Monuments of time arch across revered Lake *Kunming*.

Dazzling, serpentine marvel, a 10-kilometer covered *pavilion* promenade is restored
with over 17,000 exquisitely executed hand-painted scenes
replicated after almost total destruction
during the anti-tradition, heartless, nearly artless *Cultural Revolution*.

The *pavilion* ends at a giant marble boat, stuck in shallow, olive-colored water.
It will never set sail, ornately carved, immovable, half-immersed in the lake.
The Boat of Purity and Ease, erected in 1755, endures.

We take a ride on a small tourist dragon boat to a hilly island
where a prized concubine, one of 100s belonging to an emperor, was granted a home.

Later in the day, as we walk across the tall arch of a white-stone dragon bridge
the beauty stops me while my headphones play *Chopin*
People stare at my exotic foreignness.

III

I imagine you here with me at the *Imperial Summer Palace*
sharing 10,000 moments of happiness
in 400 different *pavilions* across the bountiful gardens and grounds.

Oblivious to counterfeit technology, military might, and the race for global dominance
brewing in the mind of the wakening dragon
I experience a lemon day of emotion, wandering in and out of towers
silvered mists feathering ancient stone steps throughout an epic history of tea and *taiji*.

In the late afternoon, near the dining room above the emerald lake
I purchase an intricate antique jade cigarette holder
from an old man who squats before tourist "antiquities"
pensively smoking rural tobacco from an old brass pipe.

Fatigued after the long day
my friends and I finally enter the palace and view treasures owned by the *Old Dowager*:

> configurations of royal-yellow silks and delicate porcelains
> imported Italian glasses, engraved brass censers
> ornaments of fine silver, tooled gold, and *cloisonné*
> fans painted with Nature scenes and poetic calligraphy
> even *ivory* sculptures, illegal to make today
> magnificent ornate mahogany benches, tables, and chairs
> screens and chests carved from rosewood and inlaid with mother-of-pearl

beauty and culture beyond the human imagination
in the past, enjoyed, hidden, and controlled by a select few.

Outside once more, with my friends, I enjoy rest, refreshment, tea, and *taiji*
in a corner near the Flowering Tree Pavilion's lotus pond.
Taiji delivers inspiration, fortitude, and awareness.
Shadow dancing in a nameless crowd, we are restored!

Our group departs for *Beida* in a yellow air-conditioned tour bus with red stripes.

Generations will continue strengthening.
Regardless of time and conditions
China offers the world ceremonious unity in tea and balance in *taiji*.

Ancient and modern, from ornate pavilions, to modest homes, to parks and gardens
shadow dancing in the shade, under the sun, or with the opal moon
people depend on balance, healing rituals of tradition, *yin* and *yang* of each passing day.

KNOWLEDGE FOR MILLENNIA

Listen to the flow of a long stream from *Qufu*
tumbling over and around the rocks of time.
Toast an abundant philosophical and material harvest.
Tip the cup of teaching. Sip the breeze of inspiration.

In the waters of the earth, wisdom is revered
respected with *stele* and ancestral graves
recorded in the *I Ching* Book of Changes.

The teacher promulgated dreams of education
with a vision of growth and change.
Cherished by generations, nurtured by wise ones
survival reproduced for millennia, silvery *Master Kong* beguiles the future.

Modern scholars converse, diverse in origins, friends in philosophy
gathering near the scholars' rocks and remembering opal moon shadows
in orchards of plum trees, a celebration of the traditions of art, teaching, and creativity.

Knowledge rises, transcends habits, fads, and mechanical life.
Redemptive bargain for the souls of the people, the words of *Confucius* still resound.

GLOSSARY

Acupuncture – An ancient Chinese medical practice using tiny thin needles at specific energy points on the body to heal a variety of ailments.

Afro-diaspora – People of African descent living outside of Africa.

Asian Studies Development Program – A program developed by the East-West Center in Honolulu for scholars and administrators to study Asian and Southeast Asian culture and history with the aim to infuse such studies into universities, colleges, and institutions of learning.

Badaguan – A section of Qingdao with European-style homes and tree-lined streets near the ocean and beaches, dating from the German occupation.

Badaling – The Chinese name of the Great Wall of China. See Great Wall.

Bai Juyi – (772-846). A renowned poet and Tang Dynasty government official who wrote of everyday life.

Ban Jeyiu – (48-6 BC). A poet, scholar, and famous woman consort during the Han Dynasty.

Banqiu – The insects known as crickets.

Baozi – Steamed buns stuffed with meats and/or vegetables.

Battle, Kathleen – A contemporary African American opera singer.

Beida – The colloquial Chinese name for Peking University. In 1898, it was established in the Haidan District of China's capital (which Westerners called Peking but in Mandarin is pronounced Beijing). It was the first modern national university in China. The picturesque campus features traditional Chinese architecture. It has over 2,000 academic staff and 30,000 undergraduate and graduate students. A center for progressive and sometimes revolutionary thought, it is an illustrious and memorable center for excellence in higher education.

Beihai Park – A large public park established in the 11th century and located in the northwest area of the Forbidden City in Beijing. Literally, *beihai* means "northern sea." Also known as Beihai Gongyuan, the imperial garden contains numerous important structures, palaces, and temples reproducing renowned scenic spots and architecture from various regions of China.

Beihuamen – The north gate. See *men*.

Beijing – The capital of China located in Hebei Province. Formerly Romanized as Peking.

Bing le –(Someone) is sick, has become sick, or was sick.

Bodhi tree – The name of the sacred tree to under which Buddhists believe under which Gautama Buddha, also known as Shakyamuni, received meditated and enlightenment. There are also actual bodhi trees with It has heart-shaped leaves that rustle in slight breeze in with a pleasant fluttering sound.

Bohai Sea – The innermost gulf of the Yellow Sea and Korea Bay on the coast of Northeastern and North China. It serves as one of the busiest seaways in the world.

Bonsai – An ancient Japanese art form dating back over 1,000 years, using trees that are grown in a tray or small container and are regularly cut and pruned to achieve certain shapes and proportions in miniature size. It is similar to the older Chinese art form called penying from which bonsai derived. The purpose of this art is for contemplation, beauty, and inspiration.

Bon voyage – "Have a good trip" or "Pleasant travels." A French expression used to say farewell and wish the traveler a good and safe journey.

Book of Changes – See Tao Te Ching.

Bourgeoisie, bourgeois – The middle class or ruling class. Sometimes used to describe and criticize those who enjoy and admire capitalism and materialistic lifestyles.

Bu yao chi fan –To not want to eat.

Capitalism – An economic system and ideology characterized by private ownership of property, free-market competition, and business for profit.

Carbonado – A black diamond, toughest form of natural diamond.

Cauchemar – A nightmare, in French.

CCTV – China Central Television. Government-sponsored and -controlled national TV. The nation's largest national broadcasting network. Includes newscasts, in-depth reports, commentary programs, and feature presentations that emphasize events in Asia and developing countries.

Central Committee – The powerful top leadership of the Chinese Communist Party. Their responsibilities include making laws; issuing policies; and controlling the military, legal systems, national treasury, international relations, and governmental investments.

Chairman Mao – See Mao Zedong.

Changcheng – See Great Wall.

Charlotte's Web – Classic American metaphorical children's book by E. B. White. Charlotte, a spider, saves the life of her friend, Wilbur, a pig, by writing lifesaving messages in her web.

Chengyang Park – A popular public park in Qingdao.

Chi – See *qi*.

Chiang Kai-Shek – Also known as Jiang Jieshi and Jiang Zhongzheng (1887-1975). The chairman of the Nationalist Party. Before the Liberation in 1949, he was the leader of China. He fled in defeat to Taiwan, where he continued as chairman of the Nationalist Party until his death.

Chi fan – To eat.

Chi fan le ma? – Would you like to eat?

Chiguo fan le ma? – Have you eaten?

Chilights – An American singing group popular in the 1970s.

Chinese New Year – The most important of the family holidays. It is based on the cycles of the moon, usually occurring in late January or early February on the first day of the lunar calendar.

Ching Dynasty – See Qing Dynasty.

Chopin, Frederic – (1810-1849). A classical Polish piano virtuoso and composer of the Romantic era who wrote primarily for the solo piano and lived in France after 1830.

Chuang – A bed.

Chuang-tzu – See Zhuangzi.

Chyn – See *qin*.

Cixi – See Old Dowager.

Class status – A system of classifying people by their economic situation or occupation. During the Cultural Revolution, these classifications were deployed as weapons of control. It was believed that one's family's class status determined one's behavior and thinking, with Red Status implying a revolutionary and acceptable person, and with Black Status assumed to be an unreliable person, an enemy who is in need of re-education, work camps, or other forms of humiliation that were often administered in public.

Cloisonné – A decorative art form in which enamel is set in hollows formed by thin strips of wire welded on a metal plate and painted.

CNTV – The national web-based broadcasting system administered by the Chinese government. It broadcasts programs in radio, film, and TV in various languages, with multiple specialty channels and subjects.

Confucius – (551-479 BC). Also known as Kong Fuzi (Kung Fu-tzu), from which the Western name, Confucius, derives; by his birth name, Kong Qiu; as well as by the honorific names Zhongni and Kongzi. Confucius was a philosopher, teacher, editor, politician, and leader of the Spring and Autumn period of Chinese history. The philosophy of Confucius emphasized personal and governmental morality, correctness of social relationships, justice, and sincerity. His followers competed successfully with many other schools during the Hundred Schools of Thought era only to be suppressed in favor of the Legalists during the Qin Dynasty. Following the victory of the Han over the Chu after the collapse of the Qin, Confucius' thoughts received official sanction and were further developed into a system known as Confucianism. Confucius' principles had a basis in common Chinese tradition and belief. He championed strong family loyalty, ancestor worship, and respect of elders by their children and of husbands by their wives. He also recommended the family as a basis for ideal government. He espoused the well-known principle "Do not do to others what you do not want done to yourself," which is similar to the Golden Rule.

Congee – A type of thick rice porridge or gruel, popular in much of Asia and believed to be good for the health, often eaten for breakfast.

Cultural Revolution – Between 1966 and 1976, under Mao Zedong, the Chinese government instituted a sociopolitical reform movement targeting perceived enemies, labeled revisionists. Schools were closed, and teenagers were authorized to abuse adults. Anyone previously in a position of power or perceived to appreciate any aspect of traditional culture was targeted. The educated were sent to work the countryside. Peasants found themselves in positions of power. Ironically, by mixing the highly educated with the illiterate farmers, Mao may have established one goal that he sought. Children of the farmers acquired the knowledge of the educated exiles, and privileged youth learned the value of physical labor, survival skills, and a respect for those who lived off the land. For a decade, the nation suffered from social and economic chaos, political purges, and millions of deaths.

Cymbidium – One of the oldest and best-known ornamental tropical Asiatic orchids producing fragrant sprays of moderate-sized flowers in a variety of colors and shades. A symbol of spring.

Daduizhang – During the Cultural Revolution, an elementary school student leader and supporter of the Communist Party doctrines, programs, and rallies, equivalent to a Student Council President.

Dantian – In *taiji* and other martial arts, a point 2 inches below the navel where one's *qi* resides.

Dao, daoism, daoist – Dao is also Romanized as tao. An indigenous wisdom tradition over 2,000 years old with an ethical philosophical tradition of Chinese origin that emphasized living in harmony with the *dao*, which means way, path, or principle. Denotes something that is both the source of and force behind everything that exists. Some people worship Laozi as the founder of the religious doctrine. The cosmological notions are taken from the School of Yin-Yang and influenced and informed by the oldest text of Chinese classics, the *I Ching*.

Dawn Cloud Sovereign – Legendary God of Taishan, said to inhabit the Peaks and to be present at dawn.

Daxue – A university.

Da Yu – (c. 2200-2100 BC). Also known as Yu the Great. Legend holds that he ruled China, introducing flood control and formalizing dynastic rule. Some maintain that the stories about him are true, first transmitted orally and later in writing. Others say that, in folklore, the Yu character originally took a different form, a god or personified animal, transforming into a human figure by the time that the stories were written down. Tales of Yu fall within the mythological era (2852-2070 BC)—with supernatural kings teaching humans about fire, housing, farming, mathematics, medicine, and writing—and the earliest recognized dynasty, the Xia Dynasty (2070-1600 BC). The oldest historical records are the oracle bones of the Shang dynasty (1600-1050 BC), and Yu does not appear on vessel inscriptions until the Western Zhou period (c. 1050–770 BC). Confucius and other Chinese teachers praised Yu and other emperors for their virtues and morals.

Dazibao – Propaganda and slogans written on large posters (often handwritten) presenting an important issue, slogan, or perspective, often used to denounce, attack, and humiliate people or the bourgeois class, especially during the Cultural Revolution.

Dharma – A term embracing philosophical or religious principle shared among Hinduism, Buddhism, and their related wisdom traditions. This word can also refer to the essential quality or character of one's own nature. Individual people make choices as to whether to conform to religious law, custom, duty, or one's own quality or character.

Ding Ling – (1904-1986). Also known by the pen name Jiang Bingzhe. One of the most celebrated 20th-century Chinese women authors. Influential in cultural circles, she was an activist, rebel, progressive, and feminist. During the Cultural Revolution, she was purged, jailed, and rehabilitated due to her views and writings. In later years, she was permitted to travel abroad, and her banned books were republished and translated.

Dingling Tomb – The mausoleum of Emperor Zhu Yijun (1563-1620), which is among the 13 Tombs of the Ming Dynasty (1368-1644).

Dong Hai Lu – The name of a street in East Qingdao, that runs downhill toward the sea.

Donghuamen – The east gate. See *men*.

Double Happiness – A brand of cigarettes.

Dragon Bay – A bay located in the Laoshan district.

Dragon Bones – Animal bones used for augury and divination.

Du Fu – (712-770). Also known as Tu Fu. A poet-sage of the Tang Dynasty, who wrote of history, morality, and sensitive feelings for humanity.

Du Mu – (803-852). A poet and government official of the late Tang Dynasty.

East-West Center – The East-West Center, established in 1960 and located at the University of Hawai`i at Mānoa in Honolulu, Hawai`i, is an independent, public, nonprofit organization. The Center aims to promote understanding among the people and nations of the U.S., Asia, and the Pacific through cooperative study, research, training, and dialogue. The Center serves as a resource for information and analysis on critical issues of common concern. Members exchange views, build expertise, and develop policy options. The Center has built a worldwide network of 62,000 alumni and more than 950 partner organizations.

8-Spoked Wheel of Law – The *dharmachakra* (Wheel of the Dharma). This iconic image is one of the Ashtamangala of Indian religions such as Jainism, Buddhism, and Hinduism. It has represented the Buddhist *dharma*. Gautama Buddha's teaching of the path to Nirvana, since the time of early Buddhism is also connected to the Noble Eightfold Path.

8 Treasures – These are simple *taiji* warm-up exercises, based on those that have been done in China for thousands of years. They are generally done early in the morning, and people of all ages do similar exercises, which are useful to relieve stress. The whole series has an overall strengthening and balancing effect on the body.

Emperor's Palace – See Forbidden City.

Erhu – A classical Chinese stringed musical instrument, sometimes called the Chinese violin or 2-stringed fiddle.

Fandian – A restaurant.

Fanzi – A house.

Faux pas – An expression in French and English meaning a misstep or an error.

Fen – A Chinese penny.

Feng shui – A Chinese philosophical system of prosperity, abundance, and health, dating from the Tang Dynasty in about 4000 BC. This system harmonizes the environment and the cosmos, creating correlations between humans and the physical world, by utilizing forces, both visible and invisible, to balance and enhance the quality of life as well as to expand awareness of a person's relation to the universe. Literally, *feng* means wind or breath and *yang* energy, conveying the idea of health; *shui* means water and *yin* energy, representing wealth and prosperity. To maximize the harmony and balance necessary to enhance social relations and interactions for a good life, the system as a philosophy applies the principles of the 4 directions and the N/S axis, historically used to create design and architectural layouts that include the 5 elements. It includes placements of doors, gates, homes, guests, plazas, temples, and tombs. It uses a system of divination to enhance the flow of positive energy, *qi*.

Feudalism – The economic system in which the majority of the land was held by relatively few landowners, who leased their vast properties to farmers and servants in return for large shares of the crops and/or service.

5 Black Categories – During the Cultural Revolution, according to Mao Zedong, the worst enemies of Communism and the common people were landlords, rich peasants, counter-revolutionaries, criminals, and rightists.

5 Blessings – The 5 traditional values held within Chinese culture: longevity, wealth, health, love of virtue, and a peaceful death.

5 Celebrated Fruits – The 5 fruits that Chinese traditionally associate with beneficence: plums, apricots, peaches, chestnuts, and dates.

5 Crest Mountain – See Taishan.

5 Elements of Feng Shui – They are earth, fire, water, air, and metal.

5 Virtues – The 5 constant virtues of benevolence, righteousness, propriety, wisdom, and fidelity are revered. Originating with Confucianism, they remain widely acknowledged. Together, they convey gravity, generosity of soul, sincerity, earnestness, and kindness.

Forbidden City – The Chinese imperial palace from the Ming dynasty to the end of the Qing dynasty, between the years 1420 to 1912. It is located in the center of Beijing and houses the Palace Museum. It served as the home of emperors and their households as well as the ceremonial and political center of Chinese government for almost 500 years. Constructed from 1406 to 1420, the complex consists of 980 buildings and covers 72 ha (180 acres).

4 Directions – The geographic directions: north, south, east, west.

4 Gentlemen of Flowers – A thematic subject/composition of traditional and modern artists who often paint plum blossoms, chrysanthemums, bamboo, and cymbidium.

4 Olds – During the Cultural Revolution, the government attempted to achieve the complete eradication of traditional Chinese culture, which the leaders categorized as old ideas, old culture, old customs, and old habits.

les Fruits de mer – In French, this refers to a variety of shell fish, usually referring to a seafood dish, either raw or cooked, and served cold on an ice-covered platter.

Fushon Bay – A small bay in Qingdao near May 4th Square.

Fuwuyuan – A server or waiter.

Gala – Slang for clams prepared in a variety of ways. *Gala* is a favorite dish in Northeast China.

Ganbei – A toast in Chinese, meaning "Bottoms Up," "Cheers," or "Drink Up."

Gao Qi – (1336-1374). A poet of the early Ming Dynasty who wrote of Nature and ordinary life.

Gingko tree – An Asiatic tree with fan-shaped leaves.

Go – Game invented in China around 3500 BC, played with black and white stones on a grid.

Gobi Desert – A desert plateau in East Asia, chiefly in Mongolia.

Goddess of Compassion – See Guan Yin.

Golden Beach – Called *Huang Dao*, this is a small island with golden sand across from Qingdao and accessible by boat.

Gongmin – A citizen of China.

Gongyuan – A park.

Great Leap Forward – From 1958 to 1961, China rapidly industrialized and collectivized. Mandatory agricultural collectivization was implemented under the directives of Mao Zedong. He emphasized punishing people rather than growing crops. It was a great leap backward. Growing crops took second place to wasteful cruelty for political purposes. Contemporary China has long expressed aversion to that period.

Great Wall – The most recognizable symbol of China and its long and vivid history, the Great Wall (Changcheng, literally, "Long Wall") actually consists of numerous walls and fortifications, many running parallel. Originally conceived by Emperor Qin Shi Huangdi (c. 259-210 BC) as a means of preventing incursions by barbarian nomads from the north into China, the wall is one of the most extensive construction projects ever completed. The best-known and best-preserved section of the Great Wall was built in the 14th through 17th centuries during the Ming dynasty (1368-1644). Though the Great Wall never effectively prevented invaders from entering China, it came to function more as a psychological barrier between Chinese civilization and the world. It remains a powerful symbol of the country's enduring strength.

Guanxi – A noun in Chinese, meaning influential connections.

Guanyin (Kwan Yin) – A Bodhisattva of mercy. Also known as a goddess of compassion, tranquility, and forgiveness.

Guizhou – Province in Southern China, famous for tea. Guizhou is a relatively poor and economically undeveloped province, but rich in natural and cultural resources. Its industries include timber and tobacco, as well as electricity generation—much of which is exported to Guangdong and other provinces—and mining of coal, limestone, arsenic, gypsum, and oil shale.

Guqin – See *qin*.

Gu Taiqing – (1799-1877). A woman poet of Manchurian descent during the Qing Dynasty.

Han Dynasty – (206-23 BC). The Han Dynasty was the second imperial dynasty of China. Founded by the rebel leader Liu Bang, who overthrew the Qin Dynasty (221-206 BC), the Han Dynasty is considered a golden age in Chinese history.

Hangzhou – A city in Southeast China, known for tea, silks, and beautiful art.

Han Yu – (768-824). A poet and essayist of the Tang Dynasty.

Hatamen – A brand of Chinese cigarettes.

Hawai`i – A group of islands located in the Pacific Ocean and the 50th state of the U.S. Popular tourist destination famous for its beautiful beaches, warm waters, and friendly people.

He cha –Would you like to have tea?

Hectare – 2.47 acres. Metric system area unit used globally for land measurement agriculture and forestry. Abbreviated with the symbol ha.

Hei – The color black.

Hei Meiguaren – Term used to refer to African Americans.

Hen gui – Very expensive, precious, valuable, honored.

Hoi Polloi – The common people, the masses.

Hong Mei – A brand of Chinese cigarettes.

Honolulu – The capital city of Hawai`i, located on the island of O`ahu. Literally, "the welcoming place."

Houston, Whitney – (1963-2012). An American singer, actor, model, and producer. In 2009, *The Guinness Book of World Records* cited her as the most-awarded female act of all time. Houston was one of pop music's best-selling music artists, with an estimated 170–200 million records sold worldwide.

Huadong Winery – Located in Laoshan Province and founded by Michael Parry, an expatriate from Britain. It has been called China's leading vineyard and is well known for its Reislings.

Huangdao – A popular island off of Qingdao, noted for its Golden Beach. Haiwan Bridge, completed in 2011, is the longest bridge over open ocean, connecting Qingdao to the island.

Huang Tingjian – (1045-1105). A poet, scholar, painter, and government official during the Song Dynasty. Sent into exile and finally settled in a daoist monastery.

Hua Tian Hotel – Located on the waterfront of Qingdao harbor and in the heart of Qingdao's business and financial district, this 4-star hotel is centrally located. It is a short walk to the famous Qingdao Pier, the central railway station, and the shopping area. It is less than an hour by car from the airport.

Hula – A graceful, slow, rhythmic dance performed for rituals and fun by the people of Hawai`i. A Polynesian dance form accompanied by chant (*oli*) or song (*mele*). It was developed in the Hawaiian Islands by the Polynesians who originally settled there. There are many sub-styles of *hula*, with the main 2 categories being *hula `auana* and *hula kahiko*. Ancient *hula*, as performed before Western encounters with Hawai`i, is called *kahiko*. It is accompanied by chant and traditional instruments. Modern *hula*, as it evolved under Western influence in the 19th and 20th centuries, is called `*auana* (which means "to wander" or "drift"). It is accompanied by song and Western-influenced musical instruments such as the guitar, the `ukelele, and the double bass.

Hutong – A cluster of narrow streets or alleys, commonly associated with Northern Chinese cities, most prominently Beijing. In Beijing, *hutong* are alleys formed by lines of traditional courtyard residences. Many neighborhoods were formed by joining one line of courtyard residences to another to form a *hutong*, and then joining one *hutong* to another. The word *hutong* is also used to refer to such neighborhoods. Since the mid-20th century, the number of Beijing hutong has dropped dramatically as they are demolished to make way for new roads and buildings. More recently, some hutong have been designated as protected areas in an attempt to preserve this aspect of Chinese cultural history.

I Ching – Also known by the title *Zhouyi*. An ancient Chinese book of divination, consisting of 64 symbolic hexagrams used to foretell the future and to indicate wise courses of action. Prescribes a system of thought on the ethics of human behaviors based on articulating cycles of change in the natural and social worlds by means of hexagrams.

Ideology – A system of beliefs.

Imperial Summer Palace – See Summer Palace.

Jia – A home or a family.

Jiali – To be at home.

Jiji Township – An area in Taiwan that suffered significant damage from the 1999 earthquake.

Jimo – A city near Qingdao in Shandong Province.

Jiaoshi – A professor.

Jiaoze – A type of dumpling or pot sticker.

Jiating – A family or household.

Jia Yi – (200-168 BC). A poet, scholar, writer, and government official who wrote about politics, education, and social and ethical ideas. His interests included ghosts, spirits, and the afterlife.

Jiayuguan – A Ming Dynasty military fort located in the Gansu corridor at the western end of the Great Wall.

Jiejie – An older sister.

Jimo – A city in Northeast China.

Jinan – The capital city of Shandong Province in Northeast China.

Jingcha – A police officer.

Jiou – Wine.

Jiu – A strong, clear alcoholic beverage.

Kang – A traditional Chinese heated platform bed made of bricks, stone, or fired clay on a long (2 meters or more) platform. Used for living, working, entertaining, and sleeping. Its interior cavity acts like a stove, providing warmth. A flue channels the exhaust from a wood or coal fire.

Karaoke – A form of interactive entertainment which an amateur singer sings along with recorded music (a music video) using a microphone and public address system. The music is typically an instrumental version of a well-known song. Lyrics are usually displayed on a video screen to guide the singer. In Asia, a *karaoke* box is called a KTV. The global *karaoke* market has been estimated to be worth nearly $1 billion.

Kong – The family name of Confucius.

Kongze – See Confucius.

Kunming Lake – The central lake on the grounds of the Summer Palace near Beijing. Longevity Hill and Kunming Lake form the key landscape features of the expansive gardens.

Lady Xu Mu. See Xu Mu.

Lancun – A city in Northeast China near Qingdao.

Laojiang – A common way to address friends or acquaintances who are older than speaker.

Laoshan – A mountainous district in Northeast China with mountains and the sea, soaring peaks, abundant vegetation, waterfalls, and large aesthetics in stone and rock. Home to the Quanzhen Dao Sect, old palaces, and sacred places. Favorite hiking and gathering places.

Laoshi – A teacher.

Lao-Tzu – See Laozi.

Laozi – Also Romanized as Lao-Tzu (d. 531 BC). An ancient Chinese writer and philosopher believed to have authored the famous *Tao Te Ching*, a commentary of the nature of existence, which offers balanced moral and spiritual guidance and is concerned with working for the good of humanity. The book speaks of the need to be flexible and observant, addressing the 4 Virtues of reverence/respect, sincerity, gentleness, and service/supportiveness.

Li – A Chinese mile, measuring .5 kilometers.

Li Bai – Also called Li Po (701-762). A revered romantic poet of the Tang Dynasty who wrote about friendship, nature, passion, love, and nostalgia, sometimes with Shamanic overtones.

Liberation – The establishment of the Chinese Communist government in 1949.

Li Po – See Li Bai.

Li Qingzhao – (1084-1151). A woman poet during Song Dynasty who wrote about love, elegant society, politics, and how humans should contribute to their country and become heroes.

Li Shangyin – (813-858). A writer of allusive poems with themes of loss and parting.

Li Shen – (d. 846). A Tang Dynasty poet and official who wrote about rural life and hard work.

Li Shizhen – (1518-1593). An influential figure in Chinese medical history. He was born during the Ming Dynasty (1368-1644), when Neo-Confucianism was rising, which significantly influenced his life. This doctrine emphasized the need for one to cultivate appropriate behavior, morality, meditation, and education. He authored the book *Bencao Gangmu*, which contains thousands of medical entries including drugs and prescriptions. Today, a well-known brand of herbs is named after him.

Li Yu – (937-978). Also known as Li Houzhu. A lyric poet and the last Emperor of the Southern Tang Dynasty, who wrote of lost love, pleasures, and regrets.

Longtan Park – Literally, "Park of the Chinese Dragon." A large public park in the Chongwen District of Beijing, just east of the Temple of Heaven, inside the 2nd Ring Road of Beijing. It contains a large central lake, Longtan Lake, which has moon bridges, rock gardens, dragon boats, tea houses, and restaurants.

Lotus – A flower said to represent purity, harmony, and integrity. It grows in muddy water but remains unstained. The root is used in cooking and is considered a delicacy.

Lu cuisine – Shandong cuisine, one of 8 culinary traditions of Chinese cuisine.

Luo Bin Wang – (619-684). A poet and Tang Dynasty official who wrote ornate verses and odes, often about the rocky political climate of his time.

Lu Xun – (1881-1936). Also known as Zhou Shuren. A leading figure of modern Chinese literature who wrote poetry and short stories in both vernacular and classical Chinese. He also worked as an editor, translator, literary critic, and essayist. After the May 4th Movement of 1919, his writing strongly influenced Chinese literature and popular culture. In the 1930s, he became the titular head of the League of Left-Wing Writers in Shanghai. After 1949, he was acclaimed by the Chinese government. Mao Zedong was a lifelong admirer of Lu Xun's writing. Though sympathetic to socialist ideas, Lu Xun never joined the Communist Party.

Lu Xun Park – A scenic park in Qingdao in honor of Lu Xun with cultural sites and views of the sea and mountains.

Lu You – (1125-1209). A poet of the Southern Song Dynasty who wrote of love, solitude, sorrow nature, family, politics, war, and death.

Lu Yu – (733-804). Author of *Classic of Tea*. He was respected as a Sage of Tea and for his contributions to Chinese Tea Culture.

Lychee – A grape-like fruit with white meat and a large brown seed. The tree is tropical and subtropical, native to Guangdong and Fujian. Today, it is cultivated in many parts of the world.

Mahjong – A game that originated in the Qing Dynasty played by 4 players with 136 or 144 tiles based on Chinese characters and symbols. The game and its regional variants are widely played throughout Eastern and South Eastern Asia and have a small following in Western countries. Similar to the Western card game rummy, *mahjong* is a game of skill, strategy, and calculation and involves a degree of chance.

Mandarin – The primary and official spoken form of the Chinese language associated with Northern China that developed under leadership of the officials in late imperial China. Based loosely on the Beijing dialect.

Mao Zedong – (1893-1976). Also Romanized as Mao Tse-Tung. Known as Chairman Mao. The son of a wealthy farmer from Shaoshan, Hunan, Mao was educated at Beida and was influenced by the Revolution of 1911 and the May 4th Movement of 1919. A nationalist and anti-imperialist, he co-founded the Communist Party of China (CPC) in 1921 and led the Autumn Harvest Uprising in 1927. He also co-founded the Red Army, which undertook a civil war against Chiang Kai-Shek's Guomindang (GMD). From 1937 to 1945, the CPC and GMD joined forces to fight the Japanese, but after that war ended they resumed fighting. In 1949, the CPC defeated the GMD, which retreated to Taiwan. On October 1, 1949, the People's Republic of China was established. From then until his death, he served as China's autocratic leader and the Chairman of the CPC. Mao is credited with modernizing China into a world power, promoting women's rights, improving education and health care, and increasing life expectancy. He is criticized for harming traditional Chinese culture and with perpetrating systematic human rights abuses such as forced labor and summary executions. His political and military theories, strategies, and policies are known as Maoism or Marxism-Leninism-Maoism. Mao solidified his power through campaigns against those called "counter-revolutionaries." In 1957, his Great Leap Forward campaign caused widespread famine and up to 45 million deaths. From 1966 to 1976, he led the Cultural Revolution, marked by violent class struggle and destruction of many cultural artifacts. In 1972, Mao met with U.S. President Richard Nixon in Beijing, an event that opened China to the West.

Master Kong – See Confucius.

Mandala – An artwork made with colored sand, or other materials such as drawings and paintings, in a circular design containing concentric geometric forms and sometimes images of deities. It symbolizes the universe, totality, or wholeness in Buddhism and Hinduism.

Maque – The birds known as sparrows.

May 4th Movement – A cultural and political movement that climaxed in Beijing on May 4, 1919. Participants protested the Chinese government's weak response to the Treaty of Versailles, especially Japan's receipt of territories in Shandong which had been surrendered by Germany. These demonstrations sparked national protests and marked an upsurge in

Chinese nationalism. Many political and social leaders of the next decades emerged at this time, including Chiang Kai-Shek and Sun Yat Sen. In a broader sense, the term refers to the period of 1915 to 1921, which is also called the New Culture Movement.

May 4th Square – Known in Chinese as Wusi Guangchang. It is a large public square in Qingdao's central business district, located between the municipal government building and Fushan Bay. It encompasses an inner central square, Shizhengting Square, and a coastal park. It contains a large May Wind sculpture. It is named after May 4th Movement.

Meiguoren – Americans, American people.

Meimei – A younger sister.

Mei Yaochen – (1002-1060). A poet and pioneer of subjective poetry who wrote of celebrations and losses in ordinary life, often with a socio-critical tone.

Men – A gate or door. In traditional Chinese architecture, the 4 directions correspond to the *men*: *donghuamen* (east), *xihuamen* (west), *shenwumen* (south), and *beihuamen* (north).

Mencius – (372-289 BC). Also called Mengzi or Meng-tzu. A Confucian philosopher born in Shandong Province. In the Warring States period, Mencius was an official and scholar at the Jixia Academy from 319 to 312 BC. Many consider him to be the most famous Confucian thinker after Confucius himself. He was an itinerant Chinese philosopher and sage, and one of the principal interpreters of Confucianism. Supposedly, he was a pupil of Confucius' grandson, Zisi. Like Confucius, according to legend, he travelled across China for 40 years, offering reform advice to rulers.

Mianbao – Bread.

Ming Dynasty – (1368-1644). Period noted for scholarly achievements and artistic works, especially porcelains.

Ming Tombs – The Ming tombs are a collection of mausoleums built by the emperors of the Ming dynasty of China. The first Ming emperor's tomb is located near Nanjing. However, the majority of the Ming tombs are located in a cluster near Beijing, collectively known as the 13 Tombs of the Ming Dynasty. The site, on the southern slope of Tianshou Mountain, was chosen according to the principles of *feng shui* by the 3rd Ming emperor. After construction of the Imperial Palace in 1420, the Yongle Emperor selected his burial site and built his mausoleum. Subsequent emperors placed their tombs in the same valley.

Moi – French for "me."

Monsoon – A seasonal wind in Southern Asia, blowing from the southwest from April to October and characterized by heavy rains.

Mount Lao – See Laoshan.

Mount Meru – A mythical sacred mountain in the cosmology of Hinduism, Jain, and Buddhism. Said to have 5 peaks and to serve as the prime axis of the world.

Mount Tai – See Taishan.

Mudra – A stylized, symbolic gesture used in dances and rituals of India, specifically an intricate movement or positioning of the hands or fingers.

Nanmu – A type of cedar wood.

Narita – An international airport near Tokyo, Japan.

Nature – Nature spelled with a capital N alludes to spirituality in everything.

Neighborhood Party Committee – In every locality, the Chinese Communist Party designates older persons as officers to mediate neighborhood and domestic disputes.

Nihao – A greeting meaning "hello."

Ni Hua Ching – (b. 1925). Known as Master Ni in his early days when teaching and lecturing the public, is now known as Grandmaster Ni, or OmNi. As a teacher of natural spiritual truth, OmNi is heir to the ancient wisdom and teaching of an unbroken succession of 74 generations in the Daoist tradition that dates back to the Han Dynasty (216 BC). He also belongs to the 38th generation of healers in the Ni family legacy. He spent his youth learning from highly achieved masters in the mountains of China. Later, he continued to study many traditions and spiritual arts from a broad range of teachers. After several decades of persistent searching and with intensive training, study, and re-examination, he moved to Taiwan in 1949. He brought the ancient wisdom (now known as the Integral Way) alive for us today by using modern language.

Old Dowager – (1835-1908). Also known as Empress Dowager Cixi. A ruthless but capable leader and the guardian aunt of the young Emperor Puyi, she essentially ran the Chinese government from 1861 until her death.

Parasol tree – A large-leafed shade tree, often found in ornamental gardens next to walls. Legend says the mythical phoenix bird will only alight in this kind of tree.

Pareo – A colorful piece of fabric worn wrapped around the body in Tahiti and Pacific Islands.

Pavilion – A part of a building or building, often partly open, connected to a group of related buildings and heavily ornamented.

Pedicab – A type of tricycle designed to carry passengers on a for hire basis. Cycle rickshaws are widely used in cities worldwide, and commonly in cities of South, Southeast, and East Asia.

Peking University – See Beida.

Pengyou – A friend.

Phoenix – A beautiful, lone, mythical bird.

Piaoliang – Pretty, good-looking, beautiful.

Pijiou – Beer.

Pinyin – The Chinese government's official Romanization system when Chinese is represented in other languages. Used in China, Malaysia, and Singapore. The International Organization for Standardization (ISO) adopted *pinyin* as an international standard in 1982.

Pipa – A 4-stringed musical instrument that is a traditional Chinese lute. It dates back 2,000 years and has a wide, dynamic range.

Proletarian – A member of the working class, especially a farmer or a factory worker.

Propaganda – Information intended to promote a particular belief. Although sometimes the word implies that the information is false or misleading, during the Cultural Revolution, it was generally considered a positive term in China.

Pu'er – Also Romanized as Puerh. A variety of fermented and aged dark tea produced in Yunnan province and named after Pu'er City. After they have been dried and rolled, the tea leaves undergo microbial fermentation and oxidation. This produces tea known as hei cha, commonly translated as dark tea or black tea (this type of tea is different from what is known in the West as "black tea," which in China is called "red tea").

Puyi – (1906-1967). Also known as Henry Pu Yi. The last Emperor of China and the 12th and final ruler of the Qing dynasty. He descended from the Manchu Aisin Gioro clan. He ruled from 1908 until his forced abdication in 1912. In 1932, after the Japanese occupied Manchuria, they installed him as the region's Chief Executive; in 1934, they named him Emperor of Manchukuo, a puppet post he held until the end of WWII in 1945. After the People's Republic of China was established in 1949, Puyi was imprisoned as a war criminal for 10 years. He wrote his memoirs and became a titular member of the Chinese People's Political Consultative Conference and the National People's Congress.

Qi (chi) – A movable life force or energy. In Chinese philosophy, *qi*, is the life force or energy that every person or thing has.

Qigong – A system of self-healing developed millennia ago in China. The practice uses breathing, posture, and concentration to balance and strengthen bodily energy systems. It aims for physical, emotional, mental, and spiritual health: aligning posture; retaining moisture; and improving blood circulation, the digestive system, and the nervous system. It promotes relaxation, concentration, balance, and alignment. These practices seek to generate the flow of *qi* throughout the body, promoting circulation, strengthening muscles, and stretching tendons. *Qigong* helps to harmonize earthly *yin* energy and heavenly *yang* energy.

Qi Dong Lu – A street in Qingdao.

Qin – Traditionally referred simply as *qin*, the *guchin* is a plucked 7-stringed zither without bridges made from wood, often bamboo. This silk-stringed instrument dates back 3,000 years. Associated with women musicians, in ages past, it was played by courtesans. It is a 7-stringed zither without bridges. It is considered the instrument of sages for the purpose of enriching the heart and elevating human nature. Confucius was a master of this instrument. In Wade-Giles Romanization, it is spelled as *chyn*.

Qing – A word meaning "please."

Qingdao – Also Romanized as Tsingtao. Located in Shandong Province, Qingdao is one of China's major coastal cities, formerly known for its sanatoriums for those suffering from tuberculosis because of the quality of the air and temperate climate. In Chinese, *qing* is "cyan" or "greenish-blue," and *dao* is "island." During WWI and WWII, the area was occupied first by the Germans and then by the Japanese. In 2014, Qingdao had a population of nearly 10 million. Located on the Yellow Sea, Qingdao is a major seaport, naval base, and industrial center. Its Jiaozhou Bay Bridge is the world's longest sea bridge, and the city hosts the second-largest brewery in China, the Tsingtao Brewery.

Qingdao University – A major research university located in Qingdao. It began in 1909 as Deutsch-Chinesische Hochschule (German-Chinese College). In 1993, the former Qingdao University, Qingdao Medical College, Shandong Textile Engineering College, and Qingdao Normal College, merged to form the new Qingdao University.

Qing Dynasty – (1644-1911). Also Romanized as Ching Dynasty and also called the Manchu dynasty since the Qing rulers were originally from Manchuria in the north.

Qin Shi Huangdi – (247-220 BC). Builder of the Great Wall, he unified China.

Qipao – A semi-sleeveless dress with a high collar and single slits on each side from knee to mid-thigh. Usually made of silk.

Quai – In French, this word means a public landing place by water. The English spelling is quay.

Qufu – The village that is associated with the birthplace of Confucius, located in Shandong Province.

Qufu Teacher's College – A public university with campuses in 2 cities: Qufu, the ancient home of Confucius, and Rizhao—both in Shandong, China. QTC's primary academic disciplines include law, education, history, calligraphy, management, chemistry, and physics.

Rampal, Jean-Pierre – A contemporary classical music flutist from France.

Red Flake – A brand of Chinese cigarettes.

Red Guards – Paramilitary social units established during the Cultural Revolution to terrorize the populace by attacking, torturing, and murdering as many older educated persons as they could find. These units consisted largely of students who were of high school and college age. The government purposely closed the schools and encouraged students to denounce their teachers as part of the ruling class and tradition.

Red Princess, Red Prince – Contemporary label for a Chinese person with high status, privileges, authority, and opportunities as a result of their parents' rank in the Communist Party.

Red Successors – Organizations in elementary schools formed in imitation of the Red Guards.

Royal – A brand of Chinese cigarettes.

Shandong Province – Shandong is an eastern coastal province influential in Chinese history, culture, and politics due to its geography along the lower Yellow River. Shandong's *Taishan* mountain is revered. It has served as a cultural and religious site for Daoism, Confucianism, and Buddhism, with the world's longest history of continuous religious worship.

Shanghai – The most populous city in China and probably the most populous city in the world. Many believe that Shanghai is the most advanced center of finance, arts, and affirmative thought.

Shenwumen – The south gate. See *men*.

Shi Lao Ren – Literally, "stone mountain," a rock in the sea just off the coast of Laoshan.

Sichuan – Also Romanized Szechwan/Szechuan, Sichuan is a province in Southwestern China well known for its special dishes and spicy cooking. The province's capital, Chengdu, is a key Chinese economic center. The area has been a major trade route from the Yellow River Valley to regions to its southwest and other areas due to its location where many water sources merge. Its name means "4 circuits of rivers and gorges."

Song Dynasty – (960-1279). This era witnessed a culture of surplus and creativity.

South China Sea – Part of the Pacific Ocean, this sea borders Singapore, the Malacca Straights, and Taiwan. As much as a third of the world's shipping travels through its waters, and it is believed to hold huge oil and gas reserves.

Stele – A stone or wooden slab erected as a monument for teaching, funerary, or commemorative purposes. Chinese steles are generally rectangular stone tablets upon which Chinese characters, poems, and philosophy are carved. There are more than 100,000 surviving stone inscriptions in China.

Struggle Meeting – During the Cultural Revolution, a meeting within a work unit to publicly criticize someone, often including humiliation or even physical assault.

Study Group – A non-official small group during the Cultural Revolution, which gathered regularly to study a particular subject, often a political issue, such as a concept or extract from Mao's works.

Su Shi – See Su Dongpo.

Summer Labor – In the Cultural Revolution period, as a regular part of their education, students took part in factory or farm work during school vacations in order to learn to appreciate the contributions of the laboring masses.

Summer Palace – Also known as the Imperial Summer Palace. In Chinese, called Yiheyuan. Located in the Haidan District of Beijing, the palace consists of many lakes, gardens, and palaces. It dates back to the Jin Dynasty in 1153. After the abdication of Emperor Puyi in 1912, the site remained owned by the Qing family. In 1914, it was opened to the public. Since 1953, it has been a major tourist attraction. In 1998, it was named a UNESCO World Heritage Site.

Su Dongpo – (1037-1101). Also known as Su Shi and Sun Tungpo. A Song Dynasty poet. He wrote philosophically about nature, travel, war, government, and politics.

Sunim, Popchong – A contemporary South Korean monk and author of the influential book *Way of Tea*.

Sun Yat-sen – (1866-1925). Universally considered to be the founder of modern China. In the Revolution of 1911, the people of China overthrew their Imperial rulers, establishing a modern republican government. He was chosen to be the nation's Provisional President.

Tai Dong – A shopping district in the older area of Qingdao with restaurants, shops, and malls. The district is known for affordable Chinese-made products.

Taiji – Also called Tai Chi, these exercises likely developed in China around the 15th century as a system of postures and meditation, characterized by slow, relaxed circular movements.

Taishan – Known in the West as Mount Tai and Mt. Tai. This is a culturally and historically significant site in Shandong Province. China is considered to have 5 Great Mountains, of which Taishan is the eastern mountain, considered primary among them and associated with birth, dawn, and renewal. Each year, millions make the pilgrimage up the 6,660 stone steps from the bottom to the top of the mountain.

Taitai – Mrs./Ms., a polite form to address a married woman or older woman.

Taiwan – Before Han Dynasty immigrants and other visitors arrived on Taiwan starting in the 17th century, the island was mainly inhabited by Chinese aborigines. After 1895, when China lost a war with Japan, the island was ceded to Japan. Japanese control ended in 1945. From 1949, the Nationalist Republic of China government lost control of China to the People's Republic of China and only held Taiwan. In 1971, the People's Republic of China replaced Taiwan on China's United Nations seat. Throughout the 1980s and early 1990s, Taiwan transitioned from a military dictatorship to a democratic multi-party elections system.

Tang Dynasty – (618-907). Regarded as a golden age, this dynasty was a time of progress and stability, ruling over tens of millions. Its capital, the city known today as Xi'an, was the most populous city in the world. The large population base allowed the dynasty to support large armies to fight Central Asian nomads and control lucrative trade routes along the Silk Road. It also exerted power over neighboring states such as Korea, Japan, and Vietnam. The dynasty maintained a civil-service system by recruiting scholar-officials through imperial examinations and official recommendations. Scholars compiled a rich variety of historical literature, encyclopedias, and geographical works. The Tang is considered the greatest age of Chinese poetry, producing the famous poets Li Bai, Du Fu, and Wang Wei. During this era, Buddhism became a major influence in Chinese culture, with native Chinese sects gaining prominence. Although the dynasty's government declined in the 9th century, Chinese art and culture continued to flourish.

Tao Qian – Also known as Tao Yuanming (365-427). A renowned nature poet who lived during the Six Dynasties period.

Tao Te Ching – Also Romanized as *Dao De Jing* and known in English as the *Book of Changes*, this famous classical book of philosophy is believed to have been written by Laozi. The oldest excavated text dates back to the late 4th century BC. Like the *Zhuangzi*, the *Tao Te Ching* is a fundamental text for philosophical and religious Daoism. It influenced other schools, such as Legalism, Confucianism, and Chinese Buddhism. Throughout the ages, Chinese artists, poets, calligraphers, and even gardeners have used this book as a source of inspiration. Its influence has spread widely, and it is among the most-often translated works of world literature.

Tao Yuanming – See Tao Qian.

Temple of Heaven – The Temple of Heaven is a medieval complex of religious buildings situated in the southeastern part of central Beijing. The complex was visited by the Emperors of the Ming and Qing dynasties for annual ceremonies of prayer to Heaven for good harvest. It has been regarded as a Daoist temple, although Chinese heaven worship, especially by the reigning monarch of the day, predates Daoism. The temple complex was constructed from 1406 to 1420 during the reign of the Yongle Emperor, who was also responsible for the construction of the Forbidden City in Beijing. The complex was extended and renamed Temple of Heaven during the reign of the Jiajing Emperor in the 16th century. In 1918, the temple was turned into a park and opened to the public. It was named a UNESCO World Heritage Site in 1998.

Thangka – Also spelled as *tangka, thanka,* or *tanka.* This is a Tibetan Buddhist painting on cotton, or silk appliqué, usually depicting a Buddhist deity, scene, or *mandala. Thangka* are traditionally kept unframed and rolled up when not on display, mounted on a textile backing like Chinese scroll paintings, with a further silk cover on the front. They must be kept in dry places to ensure longevity. Most *thangka* are small, but some are very large. Most *thangka* were intended for meditation or monastic instruction. They often have elaborate compositions with numerous small figures surrounding a central deity or spiritual figure.

3 Friends of Winter – This term refers to the plants of green pine, heavenly bamboo, and plum. They are said to encourage inspiration due to their resistance to the elements and ability to withstand hardship.

3 Plenties – This term refers to citrus fruits, peaches, and pomegranates, symbolizing abundant longevity, fecundity, and fragrance.

Tiananmen Square – A large public square in Beijing. The site of pro-democracy demonstrations in 1989, which were followed by violent government suppression.

Tiange Tea House – A tea house built in 1467 in Qingdao during the Ming Dynasty.

Tianjin – A seaport in Northeast China, this city is the capital of Hebei Province.

Tsingtao beer – Produced by the Germans from 1898 when they occupied Qingdao until the end of WW I. China's second-largest brewery.

Tu Fu – See Du Fu.

Typhoon – Any violent tropical cyclone originating in the Western Pacific, especially the South China Sea.

Waiguo – A foreigner.

Wang Bo – (650-676). A poet who wrote about friendship and advocated a style rich in emotions.

Wang Wei – (699-759). One of the most admired Nature poets with Du Fu and Li Bai. Wang was a Tang Dynasty government official and painter who wrote of nature's beauty with depth and complexity. He was named the "Poet Buddha."

Way of Tea – Cultivating tea locally, regionally and nationally for millennia, the Chinese have perfected tea manufacturing. Legend says the order to boil drinking water was given by Emperor Shennong around 3500 BC, with tea discovered in 2737 BC. Tea is associated with Daoism, Buddhism, and Confucianism, as well as literature, the arts, and philosophy. Tea drinking has been a sign of education and social status, yet, historically, in teahouses, politics and rank have been suspended in favor of the sharing of ideas while leisurely consuming tea. When Chinese people share tea together, from the humblest farmer or worker to the highest official or company leader, they participate in a valued social ritual. Every home has teaware for brewing tea, and tea is shared with visitors. The Chinese invented precious tea porcelains, and ceremonial folding of tea napkins is believed to keep away bad *qi*. Tea culture is thought to bring human beings into a higher condition of spirit and wisdom. With firewood, rice, oil, salt, soy sauce, and vinegar, tea is among the 7 Daily Necessities. The drying process begins with fresh tea leaves regularly turned in a deep bowl, which preserves the leaves' full flavor. Popular tea types include green, oolong, red, black, white, yellow, *puerh*, and flower.

Way of Tea – See Sunim, Popchong.

Weifeng – A city in Northeast China near Qingdao.

Whitney Houston – See Houston, Whitney.

Wo de jia – My house.

Wok – A large, deep cooking pan commonly used to prepare stir-fry dishes in China.

Work Unit – In China, the term used during the Cultural Revolution for any organization that employs a person.

Wo shi meiguoren – I am an American.

Wu Chang'en – (1500-1582). A poet and novelist during the Ming Dynasty who wrote of the foibles of humanity, emotions, the supernatural, and his criticism of society. He was a hermit in his later years.

Wumen Huikai – (1183-1260). A Song Dynasty poet from Hangzhou. A Buddhist monk, he famously compiled and commented on the 48-*koan* collection *The Gateless Gate*. Nicknamed "Huikai, the Lay Monk," for many years, he wandered from temple to temple, wore old and dirty robes, grew his hair and beard long, and worked in the temple fields. At age 64, he founded Gokoku-ninno temple near West Lake.

Wu Si Square – See May 4th Square.

Xiansheng – Mr., a polite form to address a man regardless of marital status or age.

Xianzai – Now.

Xiaojie – Miss/Ms., a polite form to address a single woman or younger woman. Also used for female server/waiter.

Xiao Yushan – A traditional pagoda built in 1984, it has become a modern icon in the older part of the city of Qingdao. The pagoda sits on a hill in a wooded park called Yushan Lu. The pagoda's name, Xiao Yushan, literally means "Little Yushan."

Xiexie – Thank you.

Xihuamen – The west gate. See *men*.

Xinhua News Agency – China's official, government-run press agency. Xinhua is the nation's largest, most influential media organization. Its president is a member of the Central Committee of the Communist Party. It has 31 bureaus in China and over 170 foreign bureaus. It owns numerous newspapers and a dozen magazines, which print in Chinese, English, Spanish, French, Russian, Portuguese, Arabic, and Japanese. It is the sole distributor of major news about the government and the Party. Nearly all the other Chinese media outlets rely on Xinhua for content.

Xiuxi – A nap.

Xixi – To wash up, take a bath or shower.

Xu Mu – (c. 640 BC). The first recorded woman poet in Chinese history. A princess of Wey and the first recorded female poet in Chinese history. She was married to Count Mu of Xu. Even though her surname was Ji, she became known as Lady Xu Mu, or sometimes Countess of Xu. She is known for her heroism during a civil war.

Yang – Active male energy.

Yangguizi – An offensive, derogatory term for Western foreigners, meaning foreign devils.

The Yangtze River – Known in China as Chang Jiang, literally, "Long River." It is the longest river in Asia, the third-longest in the world, and the longest within a single nation. For thousands of years, it has been used for drinking, washing, irrigation, sanitation, transportation, and industry. The river's Three Gorges Dam is the world's biggest hydroelectric power station. Prone to seasonal flooding, the river suffers from agricultural and industrial pollution and the loss of adjacent wetlands and lakes. Some sections of the river are now protected as nature reserves.

Yellow Sea – Part of the East China Sea, between China and Korea.

Yiheyuan – See Summer Palace.

Yin – Passive female energy.

Young Pioneers – A youth organization established during the Cultural Revolution for ages 6 to 14 that included most schoolchildren. Approved by the school committee, membership was intended as the first step toward eventual membership in the Communist Party.

Yuan – China's currency. Roughly the equivalent of a single US dollar, whose actual value fluctuates around 75 cents.

Yuanxiao – The Festival of Lanterns.

Yu Garden – Also called Yuyuan Garden or Garden of Happiness. Located in the older section of Northeast Shanghai near the City God Temple, these large gardens were built in the Ming Dynasty. Spirit Park, called the East Garden, was bought by local leaders in 1709. The West Garden was renovated in 1760 and in 1780. The gardens were damaged during the 19th century and again from 1956 to 1961. They were repaired by the Shanghai government in the 1970s and opened to the public. In 1982, they were classified as a national monument.

Yunnan – A mountainous and subtropical province of Southwest China, with a population of 45.7 million. Around 34% of the regional population consists of ethnic minorities. The capital is Kunming, formerly also called Yunnan. With numerous resources including aluminum, copper, lead, nickel, tin, and zinc, it also features China's greatest diversity of plant life.

Yun Yan – A brand of Chinese cigarettes.

Zaijian – Goodbye.

Zambia – A country in Southern Africa, previously known as Northern Rhodesia.

Zhanqiao Pavilion – A landmark walkway and pier in Qingdao built in 1891.

Zhanshan Temple – A famous monastery in Qingdao built in 1945.

Zhongguo – The word for "China." Literally, Middle Kingdom.

Zhongguoren – The Chinese people.

Zhongshang Park – The largest park and botanical garden in Qingdao with over 100,000 plants.

Zhongwen – The Chinese language.

Zhuangzi – (c. 369–286 BC). Also Romanized as Zhuang Tzu. A Chinese philosopher and poet who heavily influenced Chinese culture through his book of Daoist philosophy, which is titled after his name, *Zhuangzi*.

ABOUT THE AUTHOR

Kathryn Waddell Takara, PhD, is the recipient of the 2016 lifetime Achievement Award by the Honolulu NAACP as an "Agent of Change." After retiring from her position as professor of Ethnic Studies at the University of Hawai`i at Mānoa for 30 years, she pursued her career as a writer. Widely published, she has authored 8 books, and in 2012 was honored with the American Book Award for her book *Pacific Raven: Hawai`i Poems*. Takara began her second career as a publisher with her company Pacific Raven Press. She has dedicated her life to justice, peace, education, history, culture, and the environment.

Takara has coordinated several seminal national conferences on African Americans, has been a 7-time lecturer in China, and has been featured at speaking events locally, nationally, and internationally. She has published articles and been interviewed for anthologies and on television. She is active with the American Pen Women. She also is a member of The Links, Inc., and Rotary, both international organizations in service to youth, business, and the community. She raises orchids in a splendid country garden and enjoys family, travel, teaching, performing, book clubs, and mysticism.

Together with *Love's Seasons* and *Zimbabwe Spin*, the book *Shadow Dancing* completes a trilogy of her recent poetry. Looking ahead, Takara plans to publish a collection of essays, titled *Black Orchids*, about the racialization of Black women in Hawai`i; her autobiography, *Trembling Leaf: A Poet's Memoir*; and *Colonialism and Erasure: Oral Histories of Black People in Hawai`i*. She will also publish her research work on Blacks in Hawai`i.

www.ingramcontent.com/pod-product-compliance
Lightning Source LLC
Chambersburg PA
CBHW040321300426
44112CB00020B/2826